THE PRATYABHIJÑĀ PHILOSOPHY

THE PRATYABHIJÑĀ PHILOSOPHY

G.V. Tagare

MOTILAL BANARSIDASS PUBLISHERS
PRIVATE LIMITED • DELHI

First Edition: Delhi, 2002

ISBN: 81-208-1892-x

Also available at:
MOTILAL BANARSIDASS
41 U.A. Bungalow Road, Jawahar Nagar, Delhi 110 007
8 Mahalaxmi Chamber, 22 Bhulabhai Desai Road, Mumbai 400 026
120 Royapettah High Road, Mylapore, Chennai 600 004
236, 9th Main III Block, Jayanagar, Bangalore 560 011
Sanas Plaza, 1302 Baji Rao Road, Pune 411 002
8 Camac Street, Kolkata 700 017
Ashok Rajpath, Patna 800 004
Chowk, Varanasi 221 001

Printed in India
BY JAINENDRA PRAKASH JAIN AT SHRI JAINENDRA PRESS,
A-45 NARAINA, PHASE-I, NEW DELHI 110 028
AND PUBLISHED BY NARENDRA PRAKASH JAIN FOR
MOTILAL BANARSIDASS PUBLISHERS PRIVATE LIMITED,
BUNGALOW ROAD, DELHI 110 007

Contents

Preface

In India, philosophy, be it Jain, Buddhist or Vedic (Brāhmaṇical) is the basis of some pathway to Liberation (*Mokṣa*). So is *Pratyabhijñā* 'recognition', 'recognition that man or every individual soul is no other than the Supreme Soul or Parama Śiva Himself'. This inspiring concept uplifts the spirit of the down-trodden and transforms him into a dignified pilgrim on the path to *Mokṣa*. *Pratyabhijñā,* declares its formulator, is for the well-being of the common man (*janasyopakārāya*). It is true (as shown in the Introduction) that some of the concepts are anticipated by the Vedānta teacher Ādi Śaṅkara, but the credit of formulating the system goes to Vasugupta's disciple Somānanda (*circa* A.D. 825-900).

Somānanda found that the paths (*Upāyas*) to *Mokṣa*—Śāṁbhava, Śākta and Āṇava, enunciated in the *Śiva Sūtra,* are not suitable to ordinary householders as they involve Yogic exercises like Prāṇāyāma, Bandha, etc. He studied deeply the ancient *Āgamas* and discovered a *new path* (*mārgo navaḥ*). Abhinavagupta points out that the term '*navaḥ*' (New) means 'which was unnoticed till then'. Somānanda who repeated his guru's (Vasugupta's) premise of Man being Śiva himself, devised paths based on psychology. Somānanda, Utpala, Abhinavagupta, Kṣemarāja were a line of teachers who systematically developed the doctrine and practices of *Pratyabhijñā* (*circa* 900-1100 A.D.). It was briefly reviewed by the great Vedānta scholar Mādhavācārya (14th century) who subsequently occupied the post of Śaṅkarācārya at Śṛṅgeri (Karnataka).

The historical account of these teachers is briefly stated in the first chapter.

As *Pratyabhijñā* is a special branch of philosophy, it uses special technical terms, which though similar in spelling to Vedāntic terms, have a different implication. These terms are explained in the second chapter.

The third chapter explains how *"Pratyabhijñā"* system was formulated and developed by the great teachers like Somānanda, its systematic formulator, Utpala and by the great polymath Abhinavagupta of this school of philosophy.

The scholarly treatment of *Pratyabhijñā* by these teachers was beyond the capacity to understand in the case of persons who have not studied Nyāya or some such discipline. As Kṣemarāja, the author of *Pratyabhijñā-hṛdaya* (the heart or essence of *Pratyabhijñā*) states in the Introduction of his work, his book was meant for people who have not studied Dialectics and have not developed intellectual capacity to understand *Pratyabhijñā*—"for people of slow understanding" as he puts it. In fact Kṣemarāja's book is a layman's guide to *Pratyabhijñā*—as it explains both the philosophy and the different ways of Śiva realization. I have devoted chapter fourth for this important work.

Chapter fifth is the review of the *Pratyabhijñā* doctrine by the great Vedānta scholar Mādhavācārya.

The Epilogue (in addition to a brief survey of the argument) explains the relevance of *Pratyabhijñā*. We are now clearly in the 21st century.

As usual a glossary of technical terms used in the book and bibliography are supplied.

I take this opportunity to express my gratefulness to my publisher Shri N.P. Jain of the Motilal Banarsidass, Delhi for kindly allowing me the use of their publications in this book.

I sincerely thank the publisher for the beautiful production of this book.

I hope and pray "May Lord Śiva be pleased with this last Bilva leaf at His feet."

—G.V. TAGARE

Introduction

Kashmir the land of sage Kaśyapa, the domain of Nīla Nāga, is a beautiful land with snow-capped mountains, lakes with blooming lotuses, full of fragrance of sweet-scenting flowers and saffron. It is a piece of the Nandana Vana of Svarga (heaven, the abode of gods) descended on the earth. The bounteous Nature of Kashmir influenced the culture of the people and made them so tolerant and accommodative.

The *Nīlamata Purāṇa* and *Rājataraṅgiṇī,* the saga of ancient Kashmir, describe how those people followed a polytheistic religion with special veneration to Śiva and his spouse—a simple religion unencumbered with any baggage of philosophy.

It is not known when Buddhism came to be introduced in Kashmir, credit for which is given to Ashok (either of the Maurya Dynasty of Magadha or of the local Gonanda Dynasty), mentioned by Kalhaṇa in *Rājataraṅgiṇī* (I. 101-102). Kashmiris being tolerant accommodated Buddha in their pantheon.

As A. Stein noted in his introduction to *Rājataraṅgiṇī* (p.9):

> "For centuries before Kalhaṇa's time, Buddhism and the orthodox creeds existed peacefully side by side in Kashmir....of almost all royal and private individuals, who are credited with the foundation of Buddhist *Stūpas* and *Vihāras*....with equal zeal endowed also shrines of Śiva and Viṣṇu."

The peaceful coexistence of Buddhists and Śaivas continued to the end of the 2nd century A.D. When King Kaniṣka (A.D. 125-160) gifted Kashmir to the Buddhist Church, Nāgārajuna (some say Nāgabodhi)[1] energetically undertook the task of the spread of Buddhism. Practices of old local religion described in the *Nīlamata Purāṇa* were prohibited — a fact noted in the *Rājataraṅgiṇī* (I.178)[2]

This enraged Nīla Nāga, the presiding deity of Kashmir. He sent down heavy, destructive snow-fall on Kashmir. At last,

Candradeva, a Brahmin of Kāśyapa gotra, appeased the Nāga and the old religion prescribed in the *Nīlamata Purāṇa* was re-established.

Despite the attempts of Brahmins (Candradeva is their representative in the Purāṇa), the religion that was re-established lacked the pristine purity of the pre-Buddhist period. It was a harmonious mixture or amalgam of the meditative and philosophical aspect of Buddhism and the ritualistic aspect of old Śaivism. They had to accommodate Buddha in their pantheon like Brāhmaṇical Purāṇas which accepted Buddha as the ninth incarnation of Viṣṇu.[3]

We cannot, however, ascertain the nature of the Buddhist influence on the re-established Kashmir Śaivism as no scriptures of that religion are available.

It was the visit of Ādi Śaṅkara to Kashmir that gave a *coup de grace* to Buddhism in Kashmir. The visit is described in the *Śāṅkara Digvijaya* (XVI.54-80) and is confirmed by the local tradition. The visit is supposed to have taken place in the 8th century A.D., but as the note on Śaṅkara's date in the footnote 4 shows, due to Bhāvaviveka's (a Buddhist philosopher) reference to Śaṅkara's grand-teacher Gauḍapāda, Śaṅkara must be located in the 6th century A.D.

Śaṅkara, the philosopher, an advocate of Kevalādvaita in his commentary on the *Brahma Ṣūtra*, was personally a follower of the Tantric system in Śrī-cakra worship. The practice is still followed in the Śāṅkara Maṭha at Śṛṅgeri (Karnataka). He naturally introduced (sanctioned ?) the Tantra form of Śiva worship in Kashmir which was originally dominated by Śaivism. Śaṅkara's famous *stotras* (eulogies) *Saundaryalaharī* and *Dakṣiṇāmūrti* are enough to show Śaṅkara being a follower of Tantricism.

Following Dr. K.C. Pandey, I specifically mentioned the above two *stotras* as they constituted as it were the foundation of the *Pratyabhijñā doctrine* long before the ancestors of Abhinavagupta and Somānanda (the founder of *Pratyabhijñā doctrine*) migrated to Kashmir. Dr. K.C. Pandey in his standard work on *Abhinavagupta* (p.88) points out that the concept of the Ultimate Reality and important technical terms used by Śaṅkara in the above-mentioned stotras are the same as those in the *Pratyabhijñā* system.

Dr. K.C. Pandey gives the following comparison between Śaṅkara's *Dakṣiṇāmūrti Stotra* (with Sureśvara's commentary) and Utpala's *Īśvara-Pratyabhijñā -Kārikās,* to support his conjectures:

(1) *bījasyāntarīvāṅkuro jagad idam*
prāṅ–nirvikalpam punar
māyā–kalpita–deśa–kāla–kalanā-
vaicitrya–citrīkṛtam
māyāyīva vijṛmbhayatyapi
mahāyogīva yaḥ svecchayā
tasmai śrīguru–mūrtaye
nama idam srīdakṣiṇāmūrtaye.

D.M. Stotra, Verse 2

Cp.

cidātmaiva hi devontaḥ
sthitam icchāvaśād bahiḥ
yogīva nirupādānam
artha-jātaṁ prakāśayet

—Utpala, *Īśvara-Pratyabhijñā* I.182

(2) *jñāna-kriye jagat–klptau*
dṛśyete cetanāśraye

D.M. Stotra Comm. (2), Verse 13

Cp.

jñānaṁ kriyā ca bhūtānām
jīvatām jīvanam matam

—Utpala, *Īśvara-Pratyabhijñā* I.39

(3) *tasmai sattā sphurattā ca*
sarvatrāpyanuvartate

D.M. Stotra Comm. (2), Verse 13

Cp.

sā sphurattā mahāsattā
deśa–kāla–viśeṣiṇī

—Utpala, *Īśvara-Pratyabhijñā* I.207

(4) jñātṛtvam api kartṛtvam
svātantryam tasya kevalam

D.M. Stotra, V.50

Cp.

kartari jñātari svātmanyādisiddhe
maheśvare

—Utpala, *Īśvara-Pratyabhijñā* I.29

This comparison given by Dr. K.C. Pandey (in *Abhinavagupta,* p. 89) shows that Śaṅkara's visit has probably introduced these concepts in Kashmir and the Tantra-dominated worship of Śiva was either introduced or encouraged by Śaṅkara who was a Tantric worshipper. The present Tantra form of Śiva worship in Kashmir, though influenced by Vedic ritual, may be traced to the visit of Ādi-Śaṅkara to Kashmir. The continuity of the Tantra form of worship is due to the fact that Śaivism in Kashmir is Āgamic, based on Tantras and not Vedic, despite the influence of Śaṅkara and the instruction to observe outwardly Vedicism to the extent that from inception to marriage, Vedic formalities are to be observed. That Āgamic influence developed into a different schools of philosophy, the Trika philosophy, of which *Pratyabhijñā darśana* is an integral part.

Before tracing the evolution of the concept of *Pratyabhijñā* doctrine, it is necessary to know the teachers who contributed to that evolution.

Abbreviations

I.P. — Īśvara-Pratyabhijñā (Utpaladeva)

I.P.V. — Īśvara-Pratyabhijñā-Vimarśinī (Abhinavagupta)

P.H. — Pratyabhijñā-hṛdaya (Kṣemarāja)

Praty. — Pratyabhijñā

Sk. — Sanskrit

Chapter 1

Teachers of the *Pratyabhijñā* Doctrine

Very little is known about the historical development of Śaivism for two centuries or so after the visit of Ādi Śaṅkara to Kashmir. But we can presume that Śaiva Āgamas must have been composed or compiled during this period, as we find commentaries written on them from the 9th century A.D. The language of these Āgamas is similar to Purāṇic Sanskrit. Yoga, an important component part of Tantras, is post-Patañjali, the author of the *Yoga Sūtras*. They represented the Advaita, Dvaita and Dvaitādvaita Schools. It is regarded that there were ten Dvaita Āgamas and eighteen Dvaitādvaita Āgamas. But these were amalgamated before the 9th century A.D. and this combine came to be known as *Siddhānta* or *Siddhānta Śaivism*. Though Śaṅkara mentions that there were sixty-four Monistic Tantras or Āgamas at this time[1], the Advaita philosophy did not become popular. On the contrary, Siddhānta Śaivism became so popular that the Dualistic Śaivism practically swamped the Advaita School early in the 9th century. Great Dvaitī writers like Sadyojyoti, Bṛhaspati, Śaṅkaranandana wrote popular treatises on dualistic Śaivism. Sadyojyoti was called *Siddha-guru* on account of his authoritative works like *Mokṣa Kārikā, Paramokṣa Nirāsa Kārikā, Tattva Traya Nirṇaya. Bhoga Kārikā* deals with *bhoga* according to the teaching of the *Raurava Tantra* on which Sadyojyoti wrote an important commentary called *Raurava Tantra Vṛtti.*

Bṛhaspati was another great authority like Sadyojyoti. His work *Śiva-tanu-śāstra* is frequently referred to by Abhinava (Abhinavagupta) and dualistic writers like Bhaṭṭa Rāma Kaṇṭha and Aghora Śivācārya (Tamil Nadu).

Śaṅkaranandana, a dualistic Śaiva, wrote *Prajñālaṅkāra* in which he criticised the atomic theory of Naiyāyikas.

Vasugupta

In the beginning of the 9th century A.D., Siddhānta Śaivism was well-established in the valley of Kashmir. But by 825 A.D. there arose a Monistic Siddha who successfully counteracted the influence of Siddhānta Śaivism. He deeply studied the ancient monistic Āgamas and laid down three ways to liberation (*Mokṣa-mārga*) in his pithy 78 sūtras.

To give divine authority to *Śiva Sūtra,* its commentator Kṣemarāja (Kṣema), a close disciple of Abhinava, tells us a legend about the 'revelation' of the *'Śiva Sūtra'*. He (Vasugupta) may not be the author or originator but is a recorder of the sūtras.

Kṣema (Kṣemarāja), in the introduction of his commentary on *Śiva Sūtra,* tells us that the position of Monistic Śaivism in Kashmir was so critical that Lord Śiva appeared in a dream of Vasugupta and instructed him to go to a nearby hill called Mahādevagiri. There on a slab of stone are inscribed Sūtras giving the essence of Śaivism. Śiva advised Vasugupta to propagate that 'religion' among the believers. The next day Vasugupta went to that hill, Mahādevagiri and found the Sūtras inscribed on a slab of stone as told by Śiva in his dream.[2]

There is another version which says that Śiva appeared in Vasugupta's dream and instructed him in the secret teaching of Śaivism and asked him to impart to whoever was worthy to grasp that doctrine.

I believe in the second version as many saints and poets have been inspired in their dreams to write, e.g. Somānanda in Kashmir, Tukārām, the great saint-poet of Maharashtra (17th century), Coleridge's poem 'Kubla Khan'.

Vasugupta is credited to have written three works: (1) *Śiva Sūtra,* (2) *Spanda Kārikā* and (3) a commentary on the *Bhagavadgītā.* A fourth work called *Spandāmṛta* is attributed to him but at the time of editing *Spanda Kārikās* I found that *Spandāmṛta* is another name of *Spanda Kārikā.* Kallaṭa, a direct disciple of Vasugupta, calls it (the Kārikās) *'Spandāmṛta'*.[3]

1. Śiva Sūtra

Vasugupta deeply studied the Yoga sections of Monistic Āgamas and chalked out three pathways to *Mokṣa* according to the spiritual level or capacity of the aspirant to *Mokṣa*. He arranged those in descending order, the first path for a highly advanced aspirant and the last for ordinary people. They are: (1) *Śāṁbhava Upāya,* (2) *Śākta Upāya,* and (3) *Āṇava Upāya*. This *Śākta Upāya* has nothing in common with the *Śākta* sects of undesirable practices. In this *Upāya,* the power of Mantra (Śakti) is important.

2. Spanda Kārikā or Spandāmṛta

This is an amplification of the fundamental principles of Śaivism given in Sūtra form in the *Śiva Sūtra*. Kallaṭa's concluding verse of his commentary on these Kārikās confirms Vasugupta's authorship of this work.[3]

3. Commentary on the Bhagavadgītā

Abhinava's references to *Vāsavīṭīkā* (Vasugupta's commentary) on the *Bhagavadgītā* show that he must have written it, but it is not extant now. When I read Abhinava's commentary on the *Bhagavadgītā* (rightly or wrongly) I felt that Abhinava must have assimilated it.

The date of Vasugupta can be ascertained from that of his disciple Kallaṭa whom Kalhaṇa in *Rājataraṅgiṇī* V. 6, mentions as a contemporary of King Avanti Varman of Kashmir (A.D. 866-883). This means Vasugupta preceded Kallaṭa by a generation and as such may be located in circa 825-50.

It must be noted that Vasugupta established *Īśvarādvayavāda* and not the doctrine of *Pratyabhijñā*. It was for his disciple Somānanda to establish it as against different Dārśanic views current at his time. But it was creditable that undaunted by the staunch opposition, he established his Siddhānta of *Īśvarādvayavāda* which forms the fundamental principle of Pratyabhijñā.

We find Vasugupta was a spiritual founder of two branches of Monistic Śaivism—one of which is important from *Pratyabhijñā* point of view. His spiritual genealogy may be given as follows:

Vasugupta (A.D. 825-850)

Kallaṭa (disciple) (A.D. 850-900)	Somānanda (disciple) (A.D. 850-900)
Pradyumna Bhaṭṭa (a son)	Lakṣmaṇa Bhaṭṭa (a disciple, A.D. 900-950)
Mahādeva Bhaṭṭa (a son)	Abhinavagupta (a disciple, A.D. 960-1015)
Śrīkaṇṭha Bhaṭṭa (a son)	Kṣemarāja (a disciple)
Bhāskara (a disciple)	

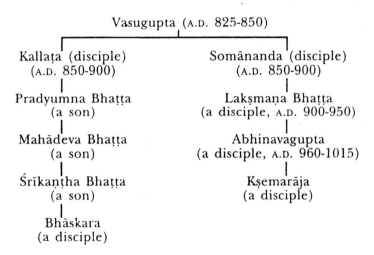

Kashmiri authors use the terms 'son' and 'disciple' indiscriminately, but I gave the genealogy as is now accepted.

One interesting feature of this Kashmir Śaivism is that the two families who contributed to the *Īśvarādvayavāda* were outsiders—non-Kashmiris. Somānanda, the founder of the *Pratyabhijñā* Doctrine came from a family of the north-eastern India. In his *Śivadṛṣti* (VII. 109-122) he narrates a semi-mythological account of his family.

It is based on the popular belief that as Āgamas are divine speech like the Vedic, like Vedas they disappear at the beginning of an evil period (for example Kaliyuga). They are not destroyed. They manifest themselves in the pure hearts of sages when auspicious times arrive.

Somānanda

Family history

At the beginning of the Kali Age, the sages who were the oral repositories of secret lores like Śaivism, retired to the village Kalāpi. It is supposed to exist somewhere in some part of the Himalaya, near Badari. It is never traced. It is probably a mythical locality. When the Śaiva lore thus disappeared, Lord Śiva (Śrīkaṇṭha) ordered sage Durvāsas to see to it that the Āgamic Śaiva lore (secret doctrine—*rahasya*) does not become extinct. Sage Durvāsas entered a spacious cave called *Tryaṁbaka*[4], created a 'mental son', designated him 'Tryaṁbaka', the name of his birthplace. The cave is known as 'Teraṁbā' in the local dialect. Sage Durvāsas commissioned him to promulgate the special Śaiva doctrine (Idealistic Monism). Tryaṁbaka, the mental son of Durvāsas, created a mental son, named him Tryaṁbaka and asked him to propagate that special Śaiva lore and flew to heaven. It was the *fifteenth* generation of mind-born teachers that took to worldly life. This mythological account shows that Somānanda had no historical information of the philosophical contribution of these Tryaṁbaka ancestors.

The last Tryaṁbaka, married a Brahmin girl and got a son 'Saṅgamāditya' from her. In course of wandering the family came to Kashmir and settled there.[5]

—*Śivadṛṣṭi* VII.114-119

Somānanda gives his genealogy from Saṅgamāditya as follows.[6]

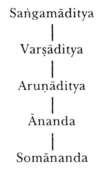

Saṅgamāditya
|
Varṣāditya
|
Aruṇāditya
|
Ānanda
|
Somānanda

Somānanda was a disciple of Vasugupta. After critically studying his teacher's work, he came to the conclusion that the three paths to liberation enunciated by Vasugupta, are difficult for ordinary people due to the rigorous discipline of Yoga and other restrictions. So he studied deeply the Āgamas and (as Lord Śiva advised him in a dream) he promulgated his doctrine of *Pratyabhijñā* which did not require the rigours of Vasugupta's paths to *Mokṣa,* and was easy to follow.[7] Though he knew that his was a new path to *Mokṣa,* he claims that whatever views are expressed by him are supported by Śāstras and have the sanction of Śiva who is all in all in everything[8] and not his own personal ones.

Somānanda: *Śivadṛṣṭi*

Somānanda states his philosophy succinctly in the first two verses of *Śivadṛṣṭi*. He offers obeisance in the *Maṅgalācaraṇa* in the third person as follows:

"Let Śiva

(1) who is one in substance with us,
(2) offer his obeisance to Śiva,
(3) who has materialized his own nature in the form of the universe,
(4) by his own power within him, and
(5) for success in overcoming the obstacles with the help of the triple agency of mind, tongue and body.

(The second verse is more specific and explanatory:)

(1) what constitutes the essence and identity of every being,
(2) what therefore self-evidently is Śiva,
(3) as continuous flow of cognition and activity,
(4) as happiness and intelligence, and
(5) as pervasive."[9]

Thus

(1) the agency used in offering the obeisance,
(2) the obstacles for removing which Śiva is praised,

Both these are consubstantial with Śiva.

Somānanda: The Darśanakāra

Before Somānanda, in Kashmiri Śaivism there was no Dārśanika work refuting the views of rival schools and establishing its stance of *Īśvarādvayavāda*. Vasugupta's *Śiva Sūtras* were dogmatic statements and *Spanda Kārikā* was its versified version. It was Somānanda who systematically presented Śaiva Monistic Idealism in a philosophical form, refuting, at the same time, other rival schools of thought in his work *Śivadṛṣṭi*. Here *dṛṣṭi* means *'darśana'* as we say *Sāṅkhya darśana, Nyāya darśana.*

The work *'Śivadṛṣṭi'* consists of seven Āhnikas or chapters presented in 700 Anuṣṭubh verses. The first four chapters have a commentary by his disciple Utpaladeva. The following are the topics discussed in these Āhnikas:

Topic discussed

Āhnika 1 (49 verses) — Gradual materialization of the Absolute Reality in concrete forms like those of animate and inanimate objects. It is a logical presentation of the process.

Āhnika 2 (90 verses) — Refutation of the theory of grammarians—the *Śabda-parabrahma-vāda.*[10] The grammarians believe in *Paśyantī* (speech) as the highest reality; it corresponds to Sadāśiva stages of the *Īśvara-pratyabhijñā.* Just as all objects are of the forms of Śiva, so is the organ of speech. That *Paśyantī* is not the highest reality[11].

Āhnika 3 (99 verses) — This deals with the refutation of the views of the Śāktas, of Śaiva Dualism (Siddhānta Śaivism) and of the Yoga philosophy. They say: "Śakti" is the real power, but for her, Śivatva is impossible. What a powerful man, if bereft of power, can do?[12]

The hypothetical bifurcation between power (*śakti*) and possessor of power, powerful (*śaktimān*) is impossible. The Śaiva position is logical. The very idea of Śiva being *śaktiless* (bereft of śakti) is unbelievable. It is by sheer will power that Śiva can do anything.

Coldness is not different from snow nor heat from fire. The *'dharma'* (characteristic) is not different from *'dharmin'* (possessor of that characteristic). Independent existence of *śakti* being untenable, Śivatva permeates all objects.[13]

Somānanda next takes up Śaiva Dualism. The opponent says: the all pervasiveness of Śiva implies amenability to change (*Vikāritva*) in Śiva.[14]

So

(1) Śiva will be inert (*jaḍa*), possessor of various limbs (*sāvayavatva*) and dependent on others (*parādhīnatva*)

(2) When everything is Śiva, there is no scope for accepting the concepts of *bandha* (bondage, *Saṁsāra*) and *Mokṣa* (liberation

from *Saṁsāra*) though this distinction is accepted by all.

(3) Exposition of (*Mokṣa*) śāstra will be meaningless.

(4) As all are (automatically) eligible for *Mokṣa*, nobody needs any advice.

(III.21-28)

Somānanda refutes (III.33 ff.):
Just as a Yogin creates by his will-power anything without any *Upādāna*, Śiva does the same by his will-power. But there is no division or partition in the body of the Yogin by his creation of an army of persons; similarly, there is no partition (*vibheda*) in Śiva's person by the creation of lower, medium or excellent objects.
Sea water raised as a wave is not called simply water but it is called a wave (*vīci*). But that does not mean the 'waterness' (*aṁbu-rūpa*) is destroyed when it becomes a wave. Similarly even in the form of an object, Śivahood (of the object) is not lost.[15]
Somānanda gives some more illustration to prove that Śivatva is not divided by a variety of objects. For example, 'Goldness' does not change with the ornaments prepared from an ingot or lump of gold.
Somānanda replies to all the objections:
To the query raised whether there are as many Śivas in the body as there are atoms comprising it. Utpaladeva, the commentator, steps[16] in and says: There is absolutely no difference in the *cid-rūpa* (universal consciousness) due to difference of time, place etc. He refers to his work *Īśvara-Pratyabhijñā* on this point.
Somānanda concludes this chapter by pointing out the difference between the concept of Īśvara in *Patañjali's Yogasūtra* and that of Śiva. With Patañjali, Īśvara is a specially gifted person who is immune from *Kleśas* (afflictions) such as *Avidyā* (nescience, ignorance), *Asmitā* (egotism), *Rāga* (desire), *Dveṣa* (hatred or aversion) and *Abhiniveśa* (tenacity of mundane existence—Monier Williams p.324 A.). Śaiva concept of God is already described above.

Proofs in support of Idealistic Monism

Āhnika 4 (124 verses) Having refuted doctrines of rival schools e.g. Vaiyākaraṇas, Śāktas, Dualist Śaivas and Pātañjala Yoga, Somānanda proceeds to delineate his philosophy : '*Everything is Śiva*', Somānanda, states in the first line of the first verse: Now (*Atha*) is to be stated that everything is Śiva (*sarvam Śivātmakam*). The first '*Atha*' is the 'seed' of what follows, for *A* stands for Śiva and *tha* represents Śakti. All objects have 'power'—each a specific one but Śiva is the real power common to all.[17] He further discusses the nature of Reality, criticises *Śūnyavāda* of Buddhists. He finally concludes the unity or oneness of the world as all objects (*bhāvas*) ultimately merge in one.[18]

The chapter appears to be incomplete because the topic ends with a half verse and there is no indication that the chapter is concluded (except in the colophon).
It is not possible even to include a summary of the chapter of the book.

Āhnika 5 (110 verses) *The identity of the nature of subjective and objective nature of the world—samatā-pratipādanam.* The topic is introduced by the query: If there can be no *samanvaya* in all objects without (i.e, in the absence of) a single principle, how came in differentiation? The concept that knowledge of an object becomes a part of the knower later expressed by Utpala and Abhinava is found here.[19]

Āhnika 6 (127 verses) Somānanda introduces the topic by stating the Śaiva position about reality and criticises the theories held by other schools such as Brahmavāda of Vedānta (vv. 4-15), the Pañcarātra theory (16-24), Arhats i.e. Jains (**25-26**), Sāṅkhyas (27), Nyāya-Vaiśeṣikas (**28-31**), Bauddhas—especially theory of momentariness (*Kṣaṇabhaṅgavāda*), *Śūnyavāda*,

Vijñānavāda (32-89), *Anekāntavāda*. It is not possible here to state the details. But Kṣemarāja, in his *Pratyabhijñā-Hṛdaya*-Sūtra 8 and the commentary[20] deals with them.

Āhnika 7 (1-106 and 107-122 verses) (Family history of Somānanda)

The esoteric doctrine which underlies spiritual powers and leads a man ultimately to liberation from Saṁsāra[21]: The secret is identification of oneself with Śiva by Japa. Even in the worship of Liṅga, the worshipper, the act of worship and the Liṅga worshipped—all these three are Śiva himself (94). Not merely worship-trio is declared as Śiva, but also the performer of sacrifice also: I am Śiva; I shall go to Śiva; *Sādhanas* for this are also Śiva.

I may quote a few concluding verses where Somānanda expresses his (or the aspirant's) identity with Śiva.[22] In the concluding verse, Somānanda tells us that he as per command of Śiva given in his dream (an echo of people's belief about *Śiva Sūtra* of Vasugupta) composed this work. The difference between the two is that Vasugupta is silent about it and Somānanda openly declares it.[23]

After completing *Śivadṛṣṭi* in an Appendix (vv. 107-122), he tells the history of his family. It is already given above. He concludes: "I have prepared a succinct treatise (*prakaraṇa*) as per my *guru's* behest, and requests his *guru* to accept this."[24]

Somānanda, presents his veiw after the refutation of rival sects. This is as follows:

"Śiva is the highest Reality. He is the essence and identity of all beings. He is *cidānanda* (consciousness and bliss). He is *svatantra*. He can create or do anything by sheer free will without the aid of any *Upādāna* (instruments, materials, etc). He manifests himself through his powers of knowledge and action."[25]

Somānanda, the first Darśanakāra of Monistic Kashmir Śaivism is hailed as the first logical exponent of *Pratyabhijñā-Śāstra*. Abhinava compliments him in the *Tantrāloka* (I.10) as:

svātmeśvara-pratyabhidhānasya tarkasya kartāraḥ

The special feature of Pratyabhijñā as a path to *Mokṣa* is that it does not involve physical exertion such a *Prāṇāyāma*, *Bandha* etc., as in Yoga, and the renunciation of the world as was expected in the pathways to *Mokṣa* detailed in Vasugupta's *Śiva Sūtra.* His disciple Utpala rightly calls it a new easy way to *Mokṣa*,'[26] Somānanda wrote a commentary on his own work *Śivadṛṣṭi.*

Abhinava informs us that Somānanda wrote a commentary on *Parā-triṁśikā* also.

Utpaladeva

Utpala, Utpaladeva or Utpalācārya was, according to Abhinavagupta, the son and disciple of Somānanda (*Tantrāloka* 37). Utpaladeva however calls himself the son of Udayākara.[27]

On the germinal ideas of the system in Somānanda's *Śivadṛṣṭi,* Utpala built a great edifice of *Pratyabhijñā* philosophy and wrote two commentaries (on his work *Īśvara-Pratyabhijñā)* viz. *Vṛtti* and *Vivṛti,* Abhinava wrote commentaries each on Somānanda's *Vṛtti* and *Vivṛti.* According to Mādhavācārya (15th century A.D.), the author of *Sarva-darśanasaṅgraha,* Somānanda's (1) *Īśvara-pratyabhijñā,* his (2) *Vṛtti,* and (3) *Vivṛti* on them and Abhi's commentary (4) *Vimarśinī* and (5) *Vivṛti-Vimarśinī* on them, constitute the *Pratyabhijñā-Śāstra.*[28] It is essentially an exposition of *Śivadṛṣṭi.* It appears that all these five treatises were available to Mādhavācārya when he wrote the section on *Pratyabhijñā-darśana.* In his *Vṛtti,* Utpala did not give any explanation of words etc. of his Kārikās. He simply stated the substance of the Sūtras or Kārikās. His aim was to state clearly what was not adequately expressed in the Kārikās[29]. It was Abhinava who tried to bring out the full import of the Sūtras implicit in their wording.

Utpala believes that man (an individual being) is essentially free as that is the very nature of man. But man does not know his Godhood due to the veil of ignorance. Recognition of one's real self is the way to regain his complete freedom, omniscience and omnipotence. The influence of Śaṅkara's views on him is already noted in the details of his work. (*Īśvara-pratyabhijñā* will be discussed later in a separate chapter.)

Utpala is credited to have written a *Vṛtti* on Somānanda's *Śivadṛṣṭi* at the request of his son. Bhāskarācārya, in his commentary *Bhāskarī* on *Īśvara-pratyabhijñā-vimarśinī* says that Utpala wrote his commentary on *Śivadṛṣṭi* before writing *Īśvarapratyabhijñā.*

But Utpala is credited to have written *Īśvara-siddhi* and its *Vṛtti Ajaḍa-pramātā-siddhi* and a *Stotrāvali* on which we have a fine commentary by Kṣemarāja.

Lakṣmaṇa Bhaṭṭa

According to Abhinava, Lakṣmaṇa Bhaṭṭa was both the son and pupil of Utpaladeva. Abhinava learnt *Darśanas, Pratyabhijñā* and the *Krama* under him. No work of Lakṣmaṇa Bhaṭṭa is discovered as yet. Abhi calls him the 'author of *Śrī Śāstra*', but nothing is known about it, nor any quotations from his work are traced by Abhinava

Abhinavagupta (990-1015 A.D.)

Abhi (Abhinavagupta), the great polymath who made a lasting contribution to Poetics, Dramaturgy and philosophy was born in the family of Atrigupta who went to Kashmir from Kānyakubja (Kanauj, U.P.) at the invitation of King Lalitāditya of Kashmir in 740 A.D. The king gave Atrigupta a mansion near Candramaulīśvara temple on the river *Vitastā* (Jhelam). Abhi's father Narasiṁhagupta alias Cukhulaka was proficient in all Śāstras and an ardent devotee of Śiva.[30] Some wrongly state Lakṣmaṇa Bhaṭṭa as Abhi's father. Dr. Pandey gives a list of some twenty teachers under whom Abhinava studied. Thus he learnt grammar from his father Narasiṁhagupta, Brahma Vidyā from Bhūtirāja, *Krama* and *Trika Darśanas* from Lakṣmaṇagupta, Dualistic Śaivism from Bhūtirāja-tanaya, *Dhvani* from Indurāja and Dramaturgy from Bhaṭṭa Tota.[31] Dr. Pandey gives a list of 41 treatises written by Abhinava. We are more concerned with his *Vimarśinī* commentary on Utpala's *Īśvara-pratyabhijñā*. He wrote another commentary on *Vivṛti* by Utpala on his above mentioned work. But *Vimarśinī* is called the smaller one (*Laghvī*) as it contains 4000 ślokas (32 syllables=1 śloka) while the bigger (*Bṛhatī*) on *Vivṛti* consists of 18000 ślokas.

We shall discuss Abhinava's *Vimarśinī* later while discussing Utpala's *Īśvara-pratyabhijñā*.

Kṣemarāja

Kṣema (Kṣemarāja) is the earliest commentator on Abhinava. In the colophons to his commentaries on Abhinava's work, he mentions himself as "Maintainer (server) of the lotus-feet of the great Ācārya Abhinavagupta-pāda."[33] This Colophon shows not merely great devotion but also close relationship to Abhinava. Dr. Pandey conjectures that as Abhinava includes 'Kṣema' in the list of his pupils in *Tantrāloka* XXXVII, it must be Kṣemarāja as Kṣemarāja, the author of *Pratyabhijñā-hṛdaya,* mentions himself as Kṣema,[34] or perhaps a nephew of Abhinava

Like Abhi, Kṣema wrote on Poetics, Tantra and Śaiva philosophy. He wrote enlightening commentaries on Tantras like the *Svacchanda, Netra* and Abhi's *Locana* (commentary on *Dhvanyāloka*). His *Spanda-sandoha* is a commentary on the first verse of the *Spanda Kārikā;* he deals with the Spanda system in it. It was followed by the *Spanda Nirṇaya,* a commentary on the entire *Spanda Kārikā.*

The most important work contributed by Kṣema to the Pratyabhijñā system, is the digest *Pratyabhijñā-hṛdaya.* It is treated in a separate chapter later. His commentary on Vasugupta's *Śivasūtra* and on Utpala's *Stotrāvali* and on *Krama-Sūtra* are well-known. In all some sixteen works are attributed to him.

Next to Abhi, Kṣema is an authority on Monistic Śaivism in general and Pratyabhijñā doctrine in particular.

Mādhavācārya

Mādhavācārya, the spiritual preceptor of Harihara and Bukka, the founders of Vijayanagar empire, was a great Kevalādvaita scholar. He ascended the *Pīṭha* of Śaṅkarācārya at Śṛṅgerī (Karnatak) *Maṭha.* In his book *Sarva-darśana-saṅgraha,* he presents the philosophical views of the then prevailing schools of Indian Philosophy from Bārhaspatyas (or Cārvākas), Nyāya-Vaiśeṣikas, Jainas, Buddhists, sects of Śaivism and ultimately, in the last chapter, proves that Advaita as enunciated by Ādi Śaṅkara is valid. In stating the philosophical tenets of Śaiva sects, Mādhavācārya, succinctly stated the Pratyabhijñā doctrine under a separate head *'Pratyabhijñā-darśana'* which I have adopted as a title for this book. Mādhavācārya profusely quotes from Abhinava and other writers on Pratyabhijñā. His review of this Darśana is translated at the end of this book.

Chapter 2

Pratyabhijñā Philosophy: Some Fundamental Concepts

Philosophy is regarded as the intellectual response of man to Nature. Though mystified in the early stages, man began to speculate whether there is any creator or controller of this world of infinite wonderful varieties or whether the world is eternal and as such there is no need to presume that it has any creator or controller. Those who believed in the existence of some such creator of the world, were called 'theists', while those who rejected this hypothesis, became known as 'atheists'. Originally these terms had no moral implication.

In India, most of the followers of the Vedas and Tantras believed that there is such a power or principle who created the world both animate and inanimate. There was another equally powerful section of thinkers consisting of Buddhists, Jainas and some followers of the Vedas like *Sāṅkhyas* and *Mīmāṁsakas* who deemed it unnecessary and illogical to conjure up some non-existent entity called God. Sages belonging to both persuasions were respectable thinkers with high moral rectitude. They shared the same values in their practical life.

Thinkers who believed that there must be some principle at the basis of the universe, called it *sat* (existential entity). Out of them who regarded this *sat* as auspicious, called it *Śiva*—the auspicious. Those who believed *sat* as 'pervading all the universe' called it Viṣṇu from Sk. $\sqrt{Vi\d{s}}$-to pervade'. Those who designated *sat* as Śiva became known as 'Śaivas' and those who named it Viṣṇu came to be known as Vaiṣṇavas. The terms 'Śaiva' and 'Vaiṣṇava' merely indicate which special characteristic attributed to *sat* happens to be acceptable to their followers.

Main Thought (currents)

In course of time, these thinkers began to investigate problems about the nature of *sat* and its relation with man and nature or the world. They came to the following three conclusions.

1. Dualists

The first natural reaction of common man: *Sat* (the existential Reality), man and the world are distinct and different *inter se.* They believed that there is some difference between:

(i) God and the individual soul,
(ii) God and matter,
(iii) the individual soul and matter,
(iv) one individual soul and another, and
(v) one material thing and another.

These are called *Pañcabhedas.* This theory emphasizes difference (*Bheda*) and hence became known as *Dvaita* (Dualism).

2. Advaita

As against this, there was another school of thought which regarded absolute non-difference, that is identity, between God, man and the world and that all these are intrinsically one and the same viz. *Sat.* This school is known as *Advaita* (Monism).

3. Qualified Non-dualism

There is a sort of compromising view between these two extremes. These thinkers believe that sentients (man, beasts, birds, etc.) are distinct from non-sentients (*Jaḍa* or the material world), but both sentients and non-sentients somehow form parts of the body or person of God. This view is called 'Qualified Non-dualism' (Viśiṣṭādvaita).

These Three Thoughts (Currents) Common to Śaivas and Vaiṣṇavas:

Monism

We find Monists among the Śaivas, the prominent among whom are the *Īśvarādvayavādins* of Kashmir. Among Vaiṣṇavas, Śuddhādvaitavādins, who do not regard Brahman as polluted by Māyā (hence *Śuddha*), are the prominent ones. More prominent than this sect is that of Ādi Śaṅkara, if we recognize him as a Vaiṣṇava due to his *Guruparaṁparā.* His spiritual tradition starts from Viṣṇu and through Brahmā-Nārada-Vyāsa-Śuka-

Gauḍapāda-Govinda-Yati (Ādi Śaṅkara's preceptor) it reaches Śaṅkara. His name misled his critics—*Vaiṣṇavācāryas*. In fact he has more claims to be Vaiṣṇava than Vallabhācārya who belongs to Viṣṇusvāmī tradition which was Raudra. Śaṅkara, despite his poetic eulogies of Viṣṇu is considered as an antagonist by Vaiṣṇava writers.

Dualism

There are dualists among Vaiṣṇavas, especially the followers of Madhva (circa 1238 A.D.). He gave a logical exposition of his system criticising Advaitism. The Śaiva dualism is called Siddhānta Śaivism—a dominant sect in Tamil Nadu.

Qualified Non-dualism

The most famous exponent of this school is Rāmānuja (1017-1127 A.D.). His *Śrībhāṣya* on the *Brahma Sūtra* is a happy blend of Vedic and Vaiṣṇava Āgama traditions. He has still a strong following in Tamil Nadu. These Vaiṣṇavas called Śrī Vaiṣṇavas criticise the dualism of Madhva philosophy, although both are Vaiṣṇavas.

Śaiva 'qualified non-dualism' is found in Śrīkaṇṭha's *Brahma-mīmāṁsā-bhāṣya*. Like Śaṅkara, he mainly depends on the exposition of the *Brahma Sūtra* and as shown by his famous commentator, Appaya Dīkṣita, he sometimes tilts to Śaṅkara's *Advaitism*.

Differences between Schools of Monism

Though the above-mentioned three patterns of thought are common to Śaivism and Vaiṣṇavism, even in the same ism there are differences of a serious nature. For example, the present work, *Pratyabhijñā-darśana* belongs to Śaiva Monism called *Trika* or *Īśvarādvayavāda*. It differs in many respects from Śaṅkara's Monism, the Kevalādvaita. The following are the main points of difference:

(i) *Īśvarādvayavāda* is based on Śaiva Āgamas. Śaṅkara's Monism is based on *Prasthāna-Trayī* (viz. ten ancient *Upaniṣads*, the *Bhagavadgītā* and the *Brahma Sūtra*).

(ii) The Brahman in Śaṅkara's philosophy (the Advaita Vedānta) is generally (and wrongly) equated with Sadāśiva of Trika Śaivism of Kashmir.

(iii) In Kevalādvaita (advocated by Śaṅkara) Māyā is indefinable or indescribable (*anirvacanīya*). If it activates Brahman for creating the universe, it (Māyā) must be real. Here we have two reals—Brahman and Māyā. This affects the position of *Kevalādvaita* which regards only Brahman as real (*Brahma satyam*). But Śiva in Kashmir Śaivism has no such need of external help. Māyā is his power (Śakti) and as such it has no independent existence (*Śakti-śaktimator abhedaḥ*).

(iv) In Kevalādvaita, the *soul* (*Ātman*) is inactive. *Buddhi* (Intelligence) which is a product of *Prakṛti* is credited with *Jīva's* activity. But in Kashmir Śaivism, Jīvātman (the soul) though limited by Malas or Pāśas, carries his five activities (*Pañca-kṛtyas*) in his own limited sphere.

(v) Kashmir Śaivism emphasizes that conferment of Śiva's grace is a condition precedent to liberation (*Mokṣa*). Learning, penance etc. of the individual is not enough. Śiva's grace is a *MUST* for *Mokṣa*. But Śaṅkara states that when Avidyā is removed by *Śravaṇa* (listening to sacred texts), *Manana* (thoughtful reflection) and *Nididhyāsana* the *Jīvātman* gets liberation. Śaṅkara's stand inspires self-confidence and has no place for servility implied in *Anugraha* (grace).

Trika Śaivism

As we have seen, it was Āgamic Śaivism that developed in Kashmir. Out of the Advaita, Dvaita and Viśiṣṭādvaita Āgamic Śaiva sects, Dvaita and Viśiṣṭādvaita sects were amalgamated before the 9th century A.D. and formed a powerful Siddhānta Śaiva sect before the time of Vasugupta (A.D. 825). Vasugupta studied deeply the sixty-four Śaiva Āgamas (at least that is the traditional number of Advaita Āgamas) and outlined three paths to liberation from *Saṁsāra.* The three fundamentals of his philosophy were: (1) Śiva or *Pati* or the Ultimate Reality, (2) Man or the individual soul or *Paśu* and (3) *Pāśa,* the bonds that reduce the original Śiva-like individual soul to the position of a *Pāśu.*

Some other explanation of the term *'Trika'* (a collection of three principles), according to the important texts, Abhinava gives these in his famous work *Tantrāloka.* This system is called Trika as the chief authoritative Āgamas are three viz. *Nāmaka, Mālinī* and *Siddhā*[1]. There are three triads in this system:

(1) *Para* (higher), (2) *Apara* (the lower), (3) *Parāpara* (the amalgamation of 1 and 2).

(1) The Para Triad—Śiva, Śakti and their union.
(2) The Apara Triad—Śiva, Śakti and Nara.

The system is called *Trika* as it deals with these triads.[2]

We are considering the Trika consisting of the (1) Ultimate Reality (Parama Śiva), (2) *Paśu* (enchained individual soul) and (3) *Pāśas* (the chains, bonds, *mala*).

Kashmiri writers regard Trika as the best one.[3]

Trika Śaiva Literature: Three divisions

The literature of the Trika system is classified into three Śāstras: (1) Āgama Śāstra, (2) Spanda Śāstra, and (3) Pratyabhijñā Śāstra

1. Āgama Śāstra

These are supposed to be revelations handed down from teacher to pupil. Their number is variously stated[4]. Some of the famous ones are *Svacchanda, Mṛgendra, Mālinīvijaya, Vijñānabhairava,* etc.

2. Spanda Śāstra[5]

Important doctrine of the system are stated herein. The important work of this Śāstra is the *Spanda Kārikā* or *Spanda Sūtra*. The principles laid down in Vasugupta's *Śiva Sūtras* are elaborated here in a versified form. It has the following commentaries:

1. *Spanda-sandoha* (com. on one Kārikā) by Kṣema (Kṣemarāja),
2. *Spanda-nirṇaya* by Kṣema,
3. *Vivṛti* by Rāmakaṇṭha, and
4. *Pradīpikā* by Utpala Vaiṣṇava.

As Utpala explains in I.P.: *Spanda* is a sort of vibratory spiritual or Brahmanic spark which appears just a moment. It is an apparent movement of what is actually steady or unmoving.[6]

3. Pratyabhijñā Śāstra

On the basis of Mādhavācārya's *Sarva-darśana-saṅgraha,* Monier Williams, in his Sk. Dictionary defines Pratyabhijñā—'Regaining knowledge or recognition (of the identity of the Supreme and the individual soul' p. 765B). The individual soul or Ātman is originally and essentially the supreme Śiva. But he was led to believe in his identity with his body (psycho-physical mechanism).

The teaching of *Pratyabhijñā*-darśana is a spiritual discipline which leads the individual to realize and get merged in the universal consciousness or supreme Śiva.

As *Pratyabhijñā* is a part of Trika Śāstra, we must know the fundamental principles of that Śāstra in order to understand *Pratyabhijñā*.

We shall briefly notice the following concepts, as these are useful to understand other works on *Trika Śaivism* as well:

(1) The Ultimate principle: *Pati: Para-Śiva*
(2) *Paśu* (*Jīvātman,* individual consciousness or self or soul)
(3) *Viśva* (the universe and its 36 components)
(4) *Pāśa, Mala, Bandha* (Bondage)
(5) *Upāya*–means of removing the Pāśas
(6) *Dīkṣā* (initiation) or *Śaktipāta*
(7) *Mokṣa* (liberation from Saṁsāra)
(8) *Svātantryavāda*
(9) *Ābhāsavāda*
(10) *Ṣaḍadhvā*

(1) Ultimate Principle: Pati: Para-Śiva

In Trika Śaivism, the Ultimate Principle is called (Para-Śiva, *cit* or *citi* (consciousness), *Parā saṁvit* (Ultimate knowledge or experience), universal consciousness, Parameśvara (Supreme Lord). The Ultimate Principle cannot be described in words or in forms. It is beyond Time and Space. It transcends the universe and also is immanent in it.

It is blissful by nature and absolutely free. The universe with its innumerable varieties is its manifestation. It is both light and enlightener. In Him there is no subject (*grāhaka*) or object (*grāhya*). It is endowed with *Prakāśa* and *Vimarśa*. The term *Prakāśa* (light, knowledge) means that which shines, and knowledge whereby manifestation of the universe takes place. The universe exists because of the *Prakāśa* of God. But if the Ultimate Principle were simply *Prakāśa*, it would have been inert (*jaḍa*) and incapable of doing anything.[8] For this, the power of *Vimarśa* is necessary to activate it. *Vimarśa* is the non-relational immediate awareness of I-ness.[9] It stands for the power which gives rise to self-consciousness, with knowledge and action. The creation, maintenance and withdrawal of the universe is due to God's power called Vimarśa.[10]

Thus, the concept of Śiva as being independent in all activities is superior to that in Śāṅkara Vedānta in which Brahman is inactive unless it is associated with Avidyā. Śaivas regard Brahman as an equivalent of Sadāśiva, the third stage lower than Śiva. *Cit* or *Citi* (consciousness) is an aspect of Śiva. The universe is created by *citi*.[11] It is non-different from Śiva as Śaivas do not admit of any difference between *Śakti* (Power) and *Śaktimat* (possessor of Power, powerful).[12] This creative power of Śiva is called *Vimarśa, Parā śakti, Parā vāk, svātantrya, sphurattā,* etc.

Thus Śiva's epithet *'Prakāśa'* means a self-refulgent illuminating principle. It is *Ahaṁ-tva* 'I-ness' (*ahaṁ-tva* or *ahan-tā*) while *Vimarśa* is the independent will-power or freedom (*svātantrya*) of Śiva. It is not contentless but just as a big *Nyagrodha* (banyan) tree is contained in its small seed, even so the universe with all the mobile and immobile beings lies in the heart of Śiva.[13]

Para Śiva has infinite powers but the following five powers are regarded as the prominent ones: *(i) Cit śakti, (ii) Ānanda śakti, (iii) Icchā śakti, (iv) Jñāna śakti,* and *(v) Kriyā śakti.*

(i) *Cit śakti:* The independent power of manifestation. It does not require any external material aid (*Upādāna*) for the creation, maintenance and withdrawal of the universe. Due to her self-dependence, she is called *svatantrā*. Utpala says: Self-consciousness is sentiency itself. It is the ever-shining independent *parā vāk* (speech). It is freedom (*svātantrya*), the supreme power of the transcendental self.[14]
Cit is *Prakāśa* (light itself, self-luminous). Śiva's self-refulgence or luminosity is *citi*. The sun shines irrespective of the existence of anything to illuminate, similarly this luminous *cit śakti* is independent of the existence of anything to illuminate.[15] It is called *Vimarśa* and *Śivatattva,* though *cit* is the characteristic nature of Śiva.

(ii) *Ānanda śakti*—the power of Bliss: As a matter of fact, *Ānanda*–Blissfulness is the nature of Śiva, although it is regarded as the power of Śiva. This power is called *svātantrya*—absolute will-power due to its capability to do anything. It too is the power full of bliss and rests within Himself–*svātma-viśrānti-svabhāva.*

In fact, *cit* and *ānanda* constitute the very nature of Śiva rather than *śaktis*. Hence Śaivas use the term *cidānandaghana* and not *sacchidānanda*. They say: unless there is *sat*–there is no basis for *cit* and *ānanda*.

(iii) *Icchā śakti* (Will-Power): The power to assume any form or to do or create anything[16]. This is absolute Free Will.[17] Hence the Lord is called *Sadāśiva* or *Sādākhya*.

(iv) *Jñāna śakti*—The power of Knowledge: Abhinava calls this *'āmarśātmakatā'*—'non-emotional' knowledge of all objects (*Īṣattayā-Vedyonmukhatā*). Due to this power, Śiva is called Īśvara.

(v) *Kriyā śakti:* Power to assume any form or create anything without extraneous help or means. Hence Śiva is called *'sad-vidyā'* or *Śuddha Vidyā*.

There are infinite modes or varieties of Power but Śiva by His will-power, manifests the universe in himself in or on his back (as there is no space outside Śiva). Somānanda, in *Śiva-dṛṣṭi* says: "Just as in the case of Yogins, variety of forms or objects is created by his sheer will-power, the Lord requires nothing more than free will to create the universe, without any external material (*Upādāna*)."[18] Somānanda's disciple and commentator Utpala endorses his views:

"That Lord, whose essential nature is sentiency externally manifests like a Yogin all the objects which are within Him, according to His Free Will, without requiring any material cause."[19]

Five Main Functions of Śiva (Pañca-kṛtyas of Śiva)

In *Svacchanda Tantra;* while offering obeisance to Lord Śiva, the five functions of Śiva are mentioned as follows:

"Salutation to the Deity who is the author (doer) of (i) creation (Sṛṣṭi), (ii) withdrawal (*saṁhāra*), (iii) concealment, (iv) maintenance of the universe, and (v) who confers Grace (and who destroys the miseries of those who pay obeisance to Him."[20]

Thus: (i) creation, (ii) maintenance, (iii) withdrawal of the world, (iv) concealment, and (v) conferment of Grace are the five functions of Śiva:

(i) *Sṛṣṭi:* From *sṛj*—'to let go', 'to manifest the world that is within Him' It is not creation but manifestation from what is within and not new creation.

(ii) *Sthiti*—To continue the process of manifestation.

(iii) *Saṁhāra*—From *saṁ* $\sqrt{}$*hṛ*, 'to take back', to withdraw. The world is not destroyed but withdrawn within by Śiva.

(iv) *Vilaya (Pidhāna):* To conceal the real nature of the individual soul.

(v) *Anugraha:* Grace. It is essential to be favoured with Lord's Grace, otherwise Mokṣa (Liberation from Saṁsāra) is impossible.

2. Paśu (Individual Soul)

All Śaiva sects whether Vedic like Pāśupata or Āgamic like Kashmir Śaivism, consider the triad *Pati, Paśu* and *Pāśa*. The term *Paśu,* for individual soul is used even in Purāṇas.

Kauṇḍinya in his *Pañcārthabhāṣya* on the *Pāśupata Sūtra* defines *Paśu* as 'one who is bound' and includes in the list of Paśus, all living beings from god Brahmā to the animal world and leaves of trees as Paśus—a view endorsed in *Liṅgapurāṇa.*[22] Kumāradeva, a dualist Śaiva, defines 'Paśu' as 'one who is bound'.[23]

The individual soul in his original status of Śiva has all his powers viz., omnipotence, omniscience, being eternally self-satisfied (*nitya-tṛpta*), eternality and omnipresence. By being bound by the *Pāśas* or *Malas* namely. *Ānava, Kārma* (pertaining to *Karmas*) and *Māyīya* (pertaining to Māyā) Paśu's powers get circumscribed. But corresponding to Śiva's powers, he retains only *Kalā* (limited energy), *Vidyā* (limited knowledge), *Rāga* (desire, limited in nature), *Kāla* (limitation in Time, span of life etc.) and *Niyati* (limitations about space and of cause).

If a person resorts to a spiritual teacher and performs penance, *yoga* etc., he can get rid of *kārma* (pertaining to *karmas*) and and Māyīya (pertaining to Māyā) Malas. It is only through the Grace of Śiva that one can get free from *Āṇava Mala.* This doctrine of Grace is as old as older Upaniṣads. Thus the *Muṇḍaka* states: "The soul cannot be attained (or visualized) by sermons, scholarship or intelligence. He reveals himself to one whom he favours."

3. Viśva (the Universe)

The universe is the manifestation of Śiva. As Śiva is real, His manifested form, the universe, is real. It is not created. *Sṛṣṭi* from $\sqrt{}$*sṛj,* to let go, is an act of bringing out what was inside

Śiva and to exhibit it on the surface of his back (as space outside Śiva is non-existent). When he takes back, draws within himself, the universe, it is called *saṁhāra, saṁ-hṛ*—to collect, to withdraw. Thus the universe is eternal. The universe is the opening out, *Unmeṣa* or expansion (*Prasāra*) of the Supreme Śiva as Śakti (his integral part). When Śiva intends to display the entire splendour of the universe that is contained in His heart, he is designated as Śakti.[24]

The Principles (Tattvas)

According to Trika Śaivism, the universe, the manifestation or expansion (*Prasāra*) of Śiva, consists of the following thirty-six principles (*Tattvas*).[25]

(1) Śiva, (2) Śakti, (3) Sadāśiva, (4) Īśvara, (5) Śuddha Vidyā (Sad-vidyā), (6) Māyā, (7) Kalā, (8) Vidyā, (9) Rāga, (10) Kāla, (11) Niyati, (12) Puruṣa, (13) Prakṛti, (14) Buddhi, (15) Ahaṁkāra, (16) Manas, (17) Śrotra, (18) Tvak, (19) Cakṣu, (20) Jihvā, (21) Ghrāṇa, (22) Vāk, (23) Pāṇi (hands), (24) Pāda, (25) Pāyu, (26) Upastha, (27) Śabda, (28)Sparśa, (29) Rūpa, (30) Rasa, (31) Gandha, (32) Ākāśa, (33) Vāyu, (34) Vahni, (35) Salila, (36) Pṛthvī.

Out of these the twenty-five principles from 12 to 36 (*Puruṣa* to *Pṛthvī*) are adopted from Sāṅkhya philosophy. Sureśvara, in *Mānasollāsa* (154) notes the group *(saṅghāta)* of thirty-six Tattvas.[26] One noteworthy point is that Śaivas have relegated Sāṅkhya Tattvas to a lower category as 'impure path' (*aśuddhādhvan*), while the remaining, those from Śiva, to Niyati. are grouped as 'pure path' (*śuddhādhvan*).

These principles can be further classified:[27]

Śuddhādhvan (Pure Path):

1-5— *Śiva, Śakti, Sadāśiva, Īśvara, Sadvidyā:*

Aśuddhādhvan (Impure Path):

(i) *Limited individual experience:* 6-11 *Māyā to Niyati* (the Kañcukas of Māyā)

(ii) *The Limited Individual:* subject-object: 12. *Puruṣa* (subject) 13. *Prakṛti* (object)

(iii) *Mental operation:* 14. *Buddhi,* 15. *Ahaṁkāra,* 16. *Manas*

(iv) *Sense-experience:*

(a) Powers of sense perception: *Jñānendriyas*
1. Smelling (*ghrāṇendriya*)
2. Tasting (*rasanendriya*)
3. Seeing (*cakṣurindriya*)
4. Touch (*sparśendriya*)
5. Hearing (*śravaṇendriya*)

(b) Powers of actions: *Karmendriyas*
1. Speaking (*vāgindriya*)
2. Handling (*hastendriya*)
3. Locomotion (*pādendriya*)
4. Excreting (*pāyvindriya*)
5. Sexual action (*Upasthendriya*)

These powers are exercised through gross physical organs.

(c) *Tanmātras* - Primary elements of perception of the particular sense-organs:
1. Sound (*śabda*)
2. Touch (*sparśa*)
3. Colour or form (*rūpa*)
4. Taste (*rasa*)
5. Smell (*gandha*)

The Tattvas of sense-experience iv(a),(b),(c) above are the products of *Ahaṁkāra*.

(v) *Material Tattvas* (32-36)

The five gross elements (*Mahābhūtas*) are the products of their respective *Tanmātras:*

(a) Ākāśa is the product of *Śabda Tanmātra*
(b) Vāyu is the product of *Sparśa Tanmātra*
(c) Tejas (Agni) is the product of *Rūpa Tanmātra*
(d) *Āpas* (water) is the product of *Rasa Tanmātra*
(e) *Pṛthvī* is the product of *Gandha Tanmātra*

All these Tattvas are *Śivarūpa.* A few remarks describing their nature are given below.

Parama Śiva is above these principles. Hence He is not included in the list of these principles.

Śuddhādhvan (Pure Path): Principles grouped under this category do not obscure.

1. Para-Śiva: In Kṣema *Parā prāveśikā;* Śiva is described as possessing the will-power and power of Prakaśa-Vimarśa while in *Ṣaṭ-triṁśat-sandoha,* he is regarded as the first creative aspect or vibration of *Parama Śiva* (*Anuttara,* the highest deity) who, as per his Free Will (*svātantrya*), wishes to manifest (let out) the universe that is within Him. This first throb (*spanda*) of Parama Śiva is the principle called Śiva.[28]

2. Śakti Tattva: Śakti,as stated in *Mālinī-Vijaya Tantra,* is the desire of Śiva to create the universe.[29] In *Parā-prāveśa Kārikā,* Śakti is the first *spanda* (vibration) of the Lord of unobstructed powers to create the world .[30] Thus *Śakti* is the kinetic aspect of Śiva. It is not different from Śiva. Śiva contains within him both subject and object (*Aham* and *Idam* aspects inseparably). But *Śakti* polarizes consciousness into *Aham* and *Idam*(I and This). Śiva is always united with Śakti both in creation and withdrawal of the universe. He is the experiencing principle, he experiences himself as Pure 'I'. All manifestation is a creative ideation of Śiva.

3. Sadāśiva or Sādākhya Tattva: Śiva's will to develop into the universe consists of two powers: Knowledge and Action. The universe is the experience of *Aham* and *Idam.* The principle called *Sādākhya* or *Sadāśiva* has both the powers viz. Knowledge and Action (*Jñānakriye sādākhyam*).

According to Somānanda there is predominance of the power of knowledge in *sādākhya.*[31] This power means, "In the experience ("I am the universe") (*Aham asmi idam*), the emphasis is on '*I-ness*'; the awareness of this (*idam*) i.e. the world, is rather vague (*asphuṭa*). Just as an artist (painter) has some vague or indistinct idea of the picture that he is going to portray, similarly the person has some vague or hazy idea or experience of the world (This-ness, *Idantā*). They call this *anunmīlita—citra Nyāya* (the manner of a picture—the outline of which is yet not clear)."[32] As Kṣema puts it, "In the *Sadāśiva Tattva,* the universe is vague (*asphuṭa*) and is dominated by a clear consciousness or experience of 'I-ness'."[33] *Sādākhya* is the first manifestation (*ābhāsa*) in which the subject (knower, perceiver) and the object (the thing perceived, the universe) are included in consciousness.

The individual who has the experience of this *Tattva* is called *Mahā-mantreśvara* and he experiences that he is the world (*Aham asmi idam*).

4. Īśvara or *Aiśvarya Tattva:* This is the next stage of development of the Divine power into the phenomenon called the world. In this *Tattva,* the manifestation of the world is more explicit. In *Sadāśiva Tattva,* the experience is 'I am this' (*Aham asmi idam*), but in Īśvara Tattva, it is 'This is I' (*Idam asmi Aham*). This is called the 'blossoming forth' (*unmeṣa*) of the world. In this *Tattva* 'I-ness' and 'This-ness' (the experiencer and the experienced, subject and the object) are equally simultaneously evident.[34] At this stage, knowledge (*Jñāna*) is dominant though the objective side of the experience i.e. universe—'This'—is clearly defined.[35] As Maheśvarānanda succinctly expresses : When the *unmeṣa* tilts inside, it is *Sadāśiva* and when it tilts outside it is *Īśvara.*[36]

The experient of the *Īśvara Tattva* is called *Mantreśvara* and he is governed by *Īśvara.*

5. Sad-Vidyā or Śuddha Vidyā: In this stage, the experience of the universe gets more distinct. I-ness and This-ness (*Ahantā* and *Idantā*) are equally balanced as two pans (with similar weights) are found equal.[37] This is called *Śuddha Vidyā.*[38] Utpala called this *Sad-Vidyā.*[39] Though the experience of the subject (*Aham*) and the object, the universe (*Idam*), in this state is distinct, they are still identified as one. This is the experience of unity-in-diversity (*bheda-abheda-vimarśanātmaka*). The experience about divinity is not obscured in these five stages. After this, in the *aśuddhādhvan* (impure path) the Divinity is not seen or experienced. As this stage is in between 'pure' and 'impure' path it is called *parāpara.*

To sum up: The development of the experience about *Viśva* is as follows:

(1&2) *Śiva Tattva* and *Śakti Tattva: Aham vimarśaḥ*/only 'I' experience.
(3) *Sadāśiva Tattva: Aham-Idam* (I-This) experience-emphasis on I-ness; mere awareness of *'this-ness.'*
(4) *Īśvara Tattva: Idam-Aham Vimarśa* (more awareness of the universe)
(5) *Sadvidyā:* equal experience of I-ness and This-ness.

Stages one to five do not obscure the vision of the Lord. Hence, they are called as forming Pure Path (*śuddhādhvan.*)

Aśuddhādhvan (Impure Path):

(6-11 Māyā and its five bodice-like coverings)

The *Tattvas* included under this head conceal the nature of the Divine.The main cause of this is Māyā and its five bodice-like coverings viz. *Kalā, Vidyā, Rāga, Kāla* and *Niyati.*

6. Māyā: Māyā is derived from *mā,* 'to measure'. The infiniteness of the experience of the Lord is delimited by Māyā. As a matter of fact, there is identity (*abheda*) in everything, but Māyā separates them and excludes one thing from another. It is owing to Māyā that the self (*Ātman*) forgets his original identity with Śiva and thinks that he (i.e. his self) and other objects are different.[40]

The individual soul being identical with Śiva has all His divine powers but they are severely circumscribed by the following *Kañcukas* (bodice-like coverings) of Māyā.

7. Kalā: It conceals the omnipotence, power to do anything or universal authority (*Sarva-Kartṛtva*), of Śiva or universal consciousness and reduces the individual soul's efficacy to a very limited extent.[41]

8. Vidyā: This reduces the omniscience (*sarvajñatva*) of the universal consciousness and circumscribes to a very great extent its capacity to know.[42-43]

9. Rāga: Śiva or the universal consciousness is perfectly self-satisfied (*pūrṇatva*) but *Rāga* creates in him a desire for something.[44]

10. Kāla: Śiva or the universal consciousness is eternal but Kāla introduces the division of Time as past, present, future.[45]

11. Niyati: The universal consciousness is perfectly free and omnipresent. *Niyati* reduces these and delimits his freedom and space.[46]

Thus the unlimited power of Śiva is limited by the *Kañcukas* of *Māyā* as follows:

The Power of Paraśiva	*Limited powers of Jīvātman*
1. Omnipotence	*Kalā*
2. Omniscience	*Vidyā*
3. Perfect self-satisfaction	*Rāga*
4. Eternity	*Kāla*
5. Free, Pervasiveness on Omnipresence	*Niyati*

The Limited Individual: Subject-Object (Puruṣa-Prakṛti)

12. Puruṣa (the subject): In Trika terminology, Puruṣa means not merely human being but includes all sentients, *Puruṣa* is Śiva who has subjected himself to the *Kañcukas* of Māyā like *Kalā, Vidyā* etc. and due to the absence of his original omniscience, omnipotence etc. got himself reduced to an atom (*aṇu*)[47]. The term *aṇu* does not signify 'space' as with other schools of philosophy but simply his limited capacity as compared with Śiva, his original status. He is, however, the enjoyer (*bhoktā*), the subjective manifestation of *Aham-asmi-idam* (I-am-the experience) of *Sadvidyā.*

13. Prakṛti: This Sāṅkhya term in Trika expresses the objective manifestation (*bhogya*). Sāṅkhyas presume one *Prakṛti* for innumerable *Puruṣas.* As contrasted with the Sāṅkhyas, in Trika, every *Puruṣa* has his individual *Prakṛti.* It expresses the objective manifestation (*idantā-vedakatva*) in the *I-This* (*aham-asmi-idam*) experience of *Sadvidyā.* It is a source of all principles beginning from *Mahat* to *Pṛthvī.* It is a state of equilibrium of *guṇas* viz. *Sattva, Rajas* and *Tamas.*[48] The guṇas are the gross forms of Śiva's powers. *Jñāna* (knowledge), *Icchā* (will) and *Kriyā* (action) cause pleasure, pain and delusion. It is the *Śāntā śakti* of Śiva.

Antaḥkaraṇa-Mental Operation (Psychic elements) 14-16:

Antaḥkaraṇa *means 'inner organ' or the psychic apparatus.* The psychic operation of cognising pleasure, pain etc, takes place by means of Tattvas Buddhi (intellect), Ahaṁkāra (ego) and Manas (Mind). Kṣema calls this triad *as* Antaḥkaraṇa.[49]

14. *Buddhi:* It is the first element issuing from *Prakṛti.* It is mental apprehension or determination (*adhyavasāya*).[50] It is the ascertaining intelligence (*Vyavasāyātmikā*) and accepts as reflections *Vikalpas* both internal (*saṁskāras*—impressions left on the mind) and external (e.g. a flask).[51] According to Trika, *Buddhi* is the power of knowledge Sāttvic in form and the decision-making power.[52]

Trika explains : Prakṛti is by itself a *jaḍa* (inert) stage in which *Puruṣa* forgets himself as if in sleep. When he wakes up, he cognises some sort of existence. The awakening is a disturbance in the balance of *guṇas* viz *sattva, rajas* and *tamas.* When one *guṇa* predominates, the other two are reduced to subordinate positions. *Buddhi* with predominance of *sattva* quality gives calm, blissful feeling, and being clear, is capable of receiving reflections of the world.

To sum up, Buddhi is the intuitive aspect of *Cit,* the power of knowledge with the capacity for determination and discrimination.

15. *Ahaṁkāra:* It is a product of *Buddhi. Puruṣa* after awakening has consciousness of his being (I-ness) and has a sense of appropriating, 'This is or is not'[53] mine'etc. It is dominated by *Rajoguṇa.*

16. *Manas: Manas* (mind) is the product of *Ahaṁkāra.* For getting knowledge of the external world, for building up perceptions, it cooperates also with the sense-organs. Hence, the creations of concepts and images (*Saṅkalpas* and *Vikalpas).*

Sense Experience:

For sense experiences, powers of sense perception (*Jñānendriyas*), powers of actions (*Karmendriyas*), and *Tanmātras* (Primary elements of perceptions etc.) are presumed.

(17-21) *Powers of sense perception*: These are the products of *ahaṁkāra.* They are as follows : The powers of

(1) Smelling (*ghrāṇendriya)*
(2) Tasting (*rasanendriya*)
(3) Seeing (*cakṣurindriya*)
(4) Feeling by touch (*sparśendriya*)
(5) Hearing (*śravaṇendriya)*

(22-26) *Powers of Action (Karmendriya)*: The following list indicates the *powers* of the organs of action and not the physical organs. These powers are derived from *Ahaṁkāra.* They are as follows: The powers of:

(1) Speaking (*Vāgindriya)*
(2) Handling (*Hastendriya*)
(3) Locomotion (*Pādendriya)*
(4) Excreting *(Pāyvindriya*)
(5) Sexual act (*Upasthendriya)*

(27-31) *Tanmātras: Tan-mātra,* 'only that much' is a term used to denote the elements of perception. These are the general elements of the particulars of sense perception. They are the products of *Ahaṁkāra*:

	Tanmātra	*Mahābhūta*	*Function*
(1)	*śabda* (sound)	*Ākāśa* (sky)	To give space
(2)	*sparśa* (touch)	*Vāyu* (wind)	To move, to re-suscitate
(3)	*rūpa* (colour, form)	*Tejas* (fire)	To burn, to digest
(4)	*rasa* (liquid)	*Āp* (water)	To satisfy (thirst etc.)
(5)	*gandha* (smell)	*pṛthvī* (the earth)	To offer support

All these *Tattvas* are created, retained and absorbed in the Omnipresent Śiva who transcends the universe.

(32- 36) *Material Tattvas*: As shown above the gross elements are the products of *Tanmātras* as given in the following table:

(Gross element) Mahābhuta	*Is produced from*	*The Tanmātra*
(1) *Ākāśa*	"	*Śabda*
(2) Vāyu	"	Sparśa
(3) *Tejas* (Agni)	"	*Rūpa*
(4) Āp	"	Rasa
(5) *Pṛthvī*	"	*Gandha*

4. Pāśa: Bandha: Mala: Bondage

The individual soul is intrinsically Śiva Himself with all his powers, but owing to his ignorance, he forgot his original Śivahood. This ignorance is called *Mala*.[54] This ignorance, which reduced him to an atom *(aṇu)* is supposed to be 'innate' ignorance pertaining to *aṇu* i.e., *āṇava Mala*. The other two bonds or *Malas* that obscure *Jīva's* powers are the *Kārma* and *Māyīya Malas*.

Here is an unanswered question: If Śiva and *Jīvātman* are identical in powers etc. how is it that *āṇava mala* enveloped the Jīvātman and not Śiva. It is explained that it is due to the Will of Śiva that the *Jīvātman* was affected by *āṇava mala* and it is through the grace of Śiva that the *ānava mala* is removed and the Jīvātman is liberated from *saṁsāra*.

So Abhinava's criticism of Śiva's wilfullness may be quoted from *Tantrāloka* (8.82). He says Śiva binds Jīvātman at his own sweet will (or of his own accord) and liberates him at his own pleasure.[55]

In fact no school of Indian philosophy has given a satisfactory explanation why God and individuals though identical, the individual is subjected to *saṁsāra.* The verbal jugglery of terms like Māyā, Avidyā etc. do not give any logical, rational explanation. Trika is no exception.

Three Bonds or Malas

Trika regard three types of Mala—*Āṇava, Kārma* and *Māyīya*

1. Āṇava: Due to Śiva's will, Jīvātman gets his universal consciousness reduced to a very limited extent. On account of that Jīvātman considers himself severed from universal consciousness—a separate individual of limited consciousness. This Mala has no beginning (*anādi*) but ends (*sānta*) through Śiva's grace.

2. *Kārma:* Due to *Āṇava Mala,* Jīvātman's powers of Knowledge, Action and Will become limited. Before the creation of the universe, Jīva's will-power is objectless. But after the creation of the world, *Jīvātman* gets a body and naturally desires to use his power of action though limited. This creates Kārma Mala.[56] This Mala is different from *Kārma saṁskāras* which are the effects or impressions resulting from acts done by thought, word and deed.

3. *Māyīya:* Māyā delimits Jīva's original powers of knowledge and action. Its *Kañcukas* obscure Jīva's original knowledge and he feels that other Jīvas and objects are different from him. This consciousness of seeing *bheda* (difference) is called *śarīra-bhuvanākāra*'[57] and he gets entangled in a series of births and deaths.

Sakala: Pralayākala: Vijñānakala

In the context of *Malas,* the above three terms are often used (1) A normal person is enveloped in these three *Malas.* He is called *sa-kala.* (2) By spiritual exertions and God's grace, the Māyīya Mala disappears but *Āṇava and Kārma Malas* remain. He does not get his original power of knowledge and action restored. He is called *Pralayākala.* For at the time of Pralaya the whole world is withdrawn by Śiva within himself and therein Māyā has no existence. But the two *Malas* persist even in that stage. Hence, such *Jīvātman* is called *Pralayākala.* Vijñānakala is free from Kārma and Māyīya Malas but not free from *Āṇava Mala.*

5. Upāyas

For getting rid of the bonds or *Malas* and securing the grace of the Lord, some spiritual discipline and prolonged efforts are necessary. These modes of spiritual discipline are called *Upāyas* for *Āveśa*.[58] (*Āveśa* is complete submergence in Śiva.) Vasugupta prescribed three Upāyas: (1) *Śāṁbhavopāya,* (2) *Śāktopāya,* and (3) *Āṇavopāya*. The *Anupāya* or *Ānandopāya* does not require any exertion on the part of the person practising this Upāya. He is spiritually so advanced that even the sight of his spiritual preceptor is enough for him for Mokṣa.

Though I have given a list of *Upāyas* as per Vasugupta's *Śiva Sūtra,* to indicate the progress of a Jīvātmā from the initial stage, the *Upāyas* are arranged here as (1) Āṇavopāya or Kriyopāya (*Upāya* with emphasis on *Kriyā);* (2) *Śāktopāya* or *Jñānopāya;* (3) *Śāṁbhavopāya* or *Icchopāya;* and (4) *Anupāya* or *Ānandopāya.* They correspond to the four powers of Śiva : *Kriyā, Jñāna, Icchā* and *Ānanda.* Kṣemarāja in *Pratyabhijñā-hṛdaya* Sūtra 18 has enumerated the following means to Mokṣa: *Vikalpakṣaya,* (corresponding to *Śāṁbhavopāya), Śakti-saṅkoca* and *vikāsa* (*Śāktopāya*), *Vāhaccheda* and *ādyanta-koṭi-nibhālana* (*Āṇavopāya*) and also meditation on the *Pañca Kṛtyas* of Śiva are the additional *Upāyas* mentioned (explained). They will be discussed later.

(1) Āṇavopāya or *Kriyopāya*

This consists of the development of *Madhya (Suṣumnā) Nāḍī* by *Japa, Prāṇāyāma,* meditation etc. It is called Bhedopāya as at the beginning, the aspirant's experience is that he (*aham*) and the world (*idam*) are different. This is called *Kriyopāya* as there is the necessity of acts like meditation, Japa, etc. Herein *Prāṇa, Manas* and the senses also are to be disciplined.

(2) Śāktopāya (Jñānopāya)

In this *Upāya,* the emphasis is on psychological practices such as meditation that I am Śiva' (*Śivo'ham*), myself i.e. I am the whole universe (*Ātmā eva idam sarvam*). Deep meditation awakens the Kuṇḍalinī power in the Mūlādhāra Cakra without much effort of breath-control and leads to self-realization. This *Upāya* starts with the distinction between 'I' and Śiva', or the Atman and the universe (*Aham-Idam*). It is hence called *Bhedopāya.* In this *manas* (mind) is pressed into service. It is called Jñānopāya because mental activities are important herein. The *Mantra śakti* in this *Upāya* helps one to attain *Prātibha Jñāna* or true knowledge. Abhinava quoted a beautiful Apabhraṁśa *dohā* for describing this *Upāya:* The black-bee *(bhramara)* i.e *Vimarśa* makes a humming sound 'I am Lord Śiva, immanent in the universe' and wears (attains) his object viz. *Prakāśa* (Divine light):[59] K.C. Pandey compares this *Upāya* with Autosuggestion.

(3) Śāṁbhavopāya

This *Upāya* is for an advanced aspirant to attain Pure consciousness (*a-kṛtrima aham)*. For this elimination of *Vikalpa* or the *bheda* concept between *This* and *That* is necessary. For the elimination of the sense of difference (*Vikalpa-kṣaya),* it is necessary to meditate on the five functions of Śiva' (*Pañcakṛtyās*) viz. creation, maintenance and withdrawal of the universe, concealment of the powers of the Self and conferment of Grace. Trika recognizes *Jīvan-mukti'* (Liberation while alive). Utpala says: "He who has realized his identity with the universe and knows that all that is manifest is simply his glory, is the highest Lord even when the determinate cognitions are still arising."[60]

When *Vikalpas* are removed and mind is concentrated gradually in due course *Īśvara*-hood (status of the Lord) is attained.[61] With this gradual removal of *Vikalpas,* the aspirant enters a stage called *Bhairavī mudrā* in which the mind is concentrated inside with eyes wide open, steady with no movement of eyelids.[62]

(4) Anupāya

An ('slight') Upāya (efforts). The *Upāya* in which there are no restrictions like meditation, worship, *Mantra,* (prescriptive and prohibitory) regulations is called *Anupāya.* The aspirant is so much spiritually advanced that by hearing a word from *guru* (spiritual preceptor) or even without a *guru,* he immediately gets Śiva's grace showered on him and he realizes his real self in a moment.[63] This is also known as *Samāveśa.*

6. Dīkṣā (Initiation): Śaktipāta: Anugraha

The word *Dīkṣā* is derived from two roots, $\sqrt{}$*dā*—'to give'and $\sqrt{}$*kṣi*—'to get destroyed'. As Abhinava defines: That in which spiritual knowledge is imparted and the bondage of *Paśu*-hood is annihilated—an act consisting of donation and destruction is *dīkṣā.*[64]

Though a spiritual preceptor(*guru*) is generally required for initiation, it is not necessary every time. By acquiring *Prātibhajñāna,* a being gets liberated, says Abhinava[65]. This descent of spiritual power (*Śaktipāta*) can be acquired even without efforts[66] (in the case of advanced souls).

This concept of Grace is as old as ancient Upaniṣads[67] like *Kaṭha* (II.3), *Muṇḍaka* (3.23). One recognizes oneself through God's Grace. For this complete submission to God (*Prapatti*) has been recommended by later Vedānta teachers like Rāmānuja.

The conferment of Grace by God (Śaktipāta) is of three types: (1) intense (2) medium, and (3) slow.

(1) Intense *(Tīvra)*: Highly advanced spiritual aspirants are blessed with intensive grace. They realize that they are free, a compact of consciousness and bliss called Śiva and the whole universe is reflected. He loses his individual consciousness in the universal consciousness. As Abhinava states in *Tantrāloka* (I.205), "The dependent Jīvātmā completely merges into Śiva"[68]. This is called *Āveśa* or *Samāveśa.*

(2) The medium *Śaktipāta* induces a person to seek a *guru,* get initiated and practice Yoga.

(3) The moderate or *Manda Śaktipāta* creates in him a desire for spiritual knowledge and meditation, Japa etc.

Thus liberation is the 'recognition' (*Pratyabhijñā*) of one's real nature or the attainment of the original, pure I-consciousness (*Akṛtrima-Aham-Vimarśa*).

Though Mokṣa is nothing but the awareness of one's true nature (*svarūpa-prathana*), it cannot be attained without the grace of Śiva or *Śaktipāta* (Descent of the Divine power) for which exertions in some form of discipline are necessary.

7. Liberation (Mokṣa)

According to Trika philosophy, "In reality bondage (*bandha*) has no existence. There is no such thing called Liberation in the absence (non-existence) of bondage", says Somānanda,[69] the founder of *Pratyabhijñā* philosophy. He argues emphatically, "As Śiva is everywhere, there is no existence of bondage and liberation. They are concepts of the ignorant."[70] The realization of our non-difference from Śiva is *Mokṣa* (Liberation) and that non-realization is bondage.[71] Abhinava states: Mokṣa is the realization of the individual soul of his being *Parāsamvit* and nothing else.[72] When this is realized contradictory words like pleasure-pain, bondage-liberation, *cit* (conscious),-*jaḍa* (inert, lifeless) become synonyms like *'ghaṭa'* and *'kuṁbha'* (both mean a pitcher) [*Tantrāloka* II.19]. When one realizes that he is Śiva or the whole universe is non-different from him, one gets the highest bliss called *Jagadānanda*.[73]

But it is important to note that one has to go through the discipline of some *Upāya* and secure God's grace for Mokṣa, the ever-present reality. As a subject (*Pramātṛrūpatayā*) he appears down to immovables. As objects he appears as external things like blue and internal (mental) feelings like pleasure, pain. etc. Apparently they appear separate while really they are not, due to the great power of *Svātantrya* (Free Will) of the Lord. This Free Will is not separate from *saṁvit* (universal consciousness). It does not conceal the real nature of the Supreme.

To sum up[74]:

Svātantrya of Supreme Lord means the power to do anything according to His Will. It is the unrestrained extension (exercise) of the Lord's Will.

8. Svātantryavāda

Svātantryavāda is a doctrine of Free Will attributed to the Supreme Lord, Parameśvara, *Cit* or Maheśvara. It is the creativity of the Supreme Reality. The designation Maheśvara implies absolute undisputed sovereignty of the Free Will. Maheśvara is *Sva-tantra.* Without the need of any external equipment *(Upādāna)*, he can create or withdraw the universe at any time with his will-power. *Svātantrya* is only a synonym of the *Avamarśa* or *Vimarśa* power of *Paraśiva.* As Śiva is supreme consciousness, he is called *Cit* or *Citi.* It is a creative flash *(sphurattā)*. As it *(Citi)* is beyond the determining or limiting factors like time, space, it is the supreme power *(Mahāsattā)*. She is called the essential heart of the Divine Lord. It is the *parā* speech (*vāk)* which ever shines independently.[75] The synonyms express various aspects of *Svātantrya.* Abhinava in his classical method of presentation describes *Svātantryavāda* as follows.[76] Parama Śiva is of the nature of consciousness. *Prakāśa* and *Vimarśa* are the constituents of that consciousness. The variety that appears in the universe is not different due to the free will (*Svātantrya)* of Saṁvit (*Universal consciousness)*.It does not conceal the nature of the supreme. Thus is *Svātantryavāda* explained.

9. Ābhāsavāda

Ā,īṣat, kiñcit, slight', -bhāsa,bhāsana, prakāśana, 'manifestation'. This doctrine is about the manifestation of the universe by the supreme. The universe is a slight manifestation of the universe that is within Para Śiva. Trika regards Para Śiva as 'the All-inclusive Universal Consciousness or Self'. The variety or differences seen in the external world are apparent. In its unmanifest state within the Lord, it is undifferentiated like the plasma in the egg of a peacock. The variegated colours of its feathers exist but in an undifferentiated stage. This called *mayūrāṇḍarasa-nyāya.*

The ultimate principle is perfect, eternally shining. It has the powers of Will, Knowledge and Action. It is both Prakāśa and Vimarśa (*Prakāśa-Vimarśamaya)*—the *Prakāśa* aspect of the ultimate is the manifestable and the manifested. But what is the relation between them? Is the manifested world real? Abhinava in *Paramārthasāra* [77] gives the analogy of a mirror and the world reflected in it. The reflection of a city etc. in the mirror is not different from the mirror but appears to be different, so the world appears different from the universal consciousness or Śiva but in reality it is not different. To quote Abhinava: "Just as in a mirror cities, villages etc. appear different from one another and from the mirror, but actually, they are not different from the mirror, similarly the world, though non-different from Parama Śiva, appears different in the variety of objects and that in universal consciousness (Śiva).

There is however, a flaw in this analogy: In the mirror, the objects reflected are different from and external to the mirror, but in the case of Parama Śiva or the universal consciousness, due to its self-consciousness, the reflection is its own ideation i.e., the world that is reflected. So self-reflection is the special feature of world-reflection in Parama Śiva. Secondly, a mirror requires external light for getting a reflection. No reflection in darkness is possible. But the universal consciousness is self-luminous. It requires no light from others as it is *Prakāśa* itself. Thirdly, a mirror is inanimate. It cannot know what is reflected in it, but universal consciousness knows its own ideation as the reflection of itself *(ātma-bhittau)*.

A better analogy is between water and its wave. Whether a wave is formed or subsided that makes no difference in the water of sea. Similarly, by the appearance or disappearance of *Ābhāsas* the underlying universal consciousness is in no way affected.

A more appropriate example is that of a Yogī. A potter or a carpenter requires external material like clay or wood (as *Upādāna)* as well as tools for their creation. But a Yogi, without any external aid or material, creates a thing simply by his sheer will-power. Similarly, the so called creation of the universe is nothing but the manifestation of the unmanifest world within Para Śiva. Utpala in *Īśvara-pratyabhijñā* says: "The essential nature of the Lord is sentiency. Like a Yogin he manifests externally all the objects which are within him according to His Free Will. For this he requires no external material cause *(Upādāna)*"[78].

In the case of Parama Śiva, the triad viz the Knower, the object of Knowledge and Knowledge itself are undifferentiated. Hence *Ābhāsa* cannot be unreal.

10. Ṣaḍadhvā

Ṣaḍadhvā means six-fold way. It is designated thus, as manifestation which is a creative descent of *Parā śakti* taking place in six ways. Hence, the term *Ṣaḍadhvā*.

At first a few technical terms need explanation:

1. *Nāda*—Basic continuum of original boundless potency.
2. *Bindu*—The condensation of *Nāda* into a dynamic control. This condensation is beyond time and space. This is the source of all manifestations. In the highest of this manifestation *Vācaka* and *Vācya* (word and the object indicated) are undefferentiated. After this, steps of creative descent begin. They are called *adhvās* (ways). They are six in number. Hence,they are collectively called *Ṣaḍadhvā*.

3. *Kalā*—At first, there develops the polarity between *Varṇa* and *Kalā*. In fact Kalā originally designates that aspect of Reality whereby it manifests its potency to create the universe. Para Śiva (the transcendental aspect of Reality) is above Kalā, as He transcends creativity and hence his attribute *'Niṣkala'*. The immanent aspect of Śiva which is related to creativity is called sakala. In *Ṣaḍadhvā, Kalā* marks a stage where things begin to differentiate from an integrated whole and as such it is an aspect of creativity. In the stage *'Parāvāk', Vācaka* (word or *śabda* index), and *Vācya* (meaning i.e *artha,* object are undifferentiated. *Varṇa* does not mean a colour or a letter of the alphabet but the functional form of the object projected from *Bindu.* "*Varṇa* connotes the characteristic measure-index of the function of the form associated with the object," explains Pratyagātmānanda Sarasvatī (quoted by Jaidev Singh) in Introduction to *Pratyabhījñā-hṛdaya* (p.21). *Varṇa* is the 'function-form' and *Kalā* is predicable.

   The second, *Adhvā* is that of *'mantra'* and *Tattva, Mantra.* The appropriate function-form or the basic formula of the next creative descent viz. *Tattva.*

   Tattva : the inherent principle or source and origin of subtle structural forms.

   The third, the last polarity is between *Pada* and *Bhuvana. Bhuvana* is the universe as it appears to apprehending centres like ourselves.

   Pada—Actual formulation of that universe by mind, reaction and speech.

The following table shows the Vācya-Vācaka relation:

Vācaka or *śabda*	*Vācya* or *Artha*
1. Varṇa	*Kalā*
2. Mantra	*Tattva*
3. *Pada*	*Bhuvana*

Out of the two triads, the *Vācaka* or *śabda* triad (*Varṇa, Mantra* and *Pada)* is called *Kālādhvā* and the triad of *Vācya* (*Kalā, Tattva* and *Bhuvana)* is called *Deśādhvā.* Out of these, *Varṇādhvā* is of the nature of *Pramā.* In it rest *Prameya* (object), *Pramāṇa* (means of knowledge) and *Pramātā* (the experiencing soul, experient).

Varṇa is of two kinds : *Non-māyīya* and *Māyīya*. Māyīya Varṇas arise out of non-Māyīya. The non-Māyīya Varṇas are pure, natural, innumerable and without limitation. The *Vācaka śakti* (indicative power) of non-Māyīya Varṇas is inherent in the Māyīya *Varṇas* just as the power of heating is inherent in fire. The whole of this discussion is esoteric and is based on the works of Abhinava and of Jaidev Singh and others.

Five Kalās of Śiva :

Abhinava describes the following *Kalās* (phases)and the *Bhuvanas* they contain :

1. *Nivṛtti Kalā*—It is formed mainly of the *Pṛthvī Tattva* and has 16 *Bhuvanas* or planes of existence. The lowest plane of this Kalā is called Kālāgni Rudra Bhuvana. This *Kalā* is the last *Kalā*.
2. *Pratiṣṭhā Kalā*—The second *Kalā* is above *Nivṛtti Kalā*. It has 23 *Tattvas* from *Jala Tattva* upto *Prakṛti Tattva* and consists of 56 *Bhuvanas*.
3. *Vidyā Kalā*—It is above *Pratiṣṭhā Kalā*. It contains seven *Tattvas* from *Puruṣa* to *Māyā* and has 28 *Bhuvanas*.
4. *Śāntā Kalā*—This Kalā has three *Tattvas* viz. *Śuddha Vidyā*, *Īśvara* and *Sadāśiva* and 18 *Bhuvanas*.
5. *Śāntātīta Kalā*—This Kalā consists of *Śiva śakti* Tattvas and has no Bhuvana. Parama Śiva transcends all the *Kalās*. The number of *Bhuvanas* (according to Abhinava) is 118.

Chapter 3

Īśvara-Pratyabhijñā-Vimarśinī (Introductory Note)

As stated in the introduction, *Īśvara-Pratyabhijñā-Vimarśinī* (IPV) is a commentary by Abhinavagupta on *Īśvara-Pratyabhijñā* (IP) by Utpala. The credit of finding a new method or path to Mokṣa or merging in the Universal Consciousness, goes to Somānanda who took into account the difficulties of common man in adopting the three Upāyas *(Śāmbhava, Śākta* and *Āṇava)* for attainment of liberation and advocated a path—a psychological-cum-spiritual one for the merger of the individual soul into the universal consciousness (Liberation, Mokṣa). The path of *Pratyabhijñā* does not prescribe breath-control (*Prāṇāyāma*), *Bandha* and such other exertions. Therefore, there is no boast or exaggeration when Utpala claims that *Pratyabhijñā* is an easy novel way to Mokṣa.[1]

sughaṭa eṣa mārgo navo (IP, IV 1.16)

Utpala devoted some 21-22 Kārikās to state his doctrine of *Pratyabhijñā*. It is to the credit of his (Utpala's) disciple Abhinavagupta to create a majestic structure of *Pratyabhijñā*, even while assuming a low profile of a commentator of IP. Scholars who try to give faithful literal translation of old polemic works, produce a work of long compounds, involved constructions and an unfamiliar method of argumentation. In order to invite and retain the attention and interest in an esoteric subject like *Pratyabhijñā*. I have decided to present a *summary* of Abhinava's commentary in a readable form. I have not omitted a single point from Abhinava's exposition of the Text.

The text of *Pratyabhijñā-Vimarśinī* i.e., Abhinavagupta's commentary along with the Sanskrit (transliterated Text of Utpala) is presented in the hope that the translation of this *dārśanika* Text will be useful even to lay readers.

Abhi's Introduction

Like other Darśana writers, Abhinava states the gist of his views in the first benedictory verse (Maṅgalācaraṇa).[2] It succinctly gives his concept of the 'Supreme Reality', Parama Śiva:

(1) Parama Śiva is the Absolute.
(2) It is the Unity of Parama Śiva and Śakti.
(3) From this Ultimate state, first of all manifested Pure Ego, 'Í' (when there was no differentiation like Śiva and Śakti).
(4) He divides His power in two, through His Will.
(5) He is self-contained.
(6) He is the Ultimate state (but) without being manifest.
(7) He creates and withdraws (dissolves) through the exercise (play) and suspension (withdrawal of His powers).

The salutation is to that non-dual (advaita) of Parama Śiva and Śakti.

Self-Introduction

Abhinava introduces himself as the son of Lakṣmaṇagupta and the grand-disciple (disciple's disciples) of Utpala, the author of *Īśvara-Pratyabhijñā* (IP). He (Abhinava) is commenting on the above work which is a representative of the work of Somānanda (viz. *Śiva-dṛṣṭi*). Though Utpala has written a commentary *(Vṛtti)* on the IP, he (Abhinava) wishes to elucidate the conception to all people. He hopes that his exposition (of IP) will help all people of both of keen and slow understanding, if none else at least to himself[3] (that is 'his sons and disciples'—Bhāskara, the commentator of Abhinava).

Aim of Work

The author is confident of his own Śiva-realization. He wishes to transfer similar identification with Śiva, to others. He declares his object in a verse:[4] "I have anyhow realized my identification with the Supreme (Para Śiva). I wish to render service to humanity. With this aim in view, I establish *Pratyabhijñā* as that alone is the means (path) of attaining the most valuable (i.e. Mokṣa)".

In this verse, the statement of the object occupies a subordinate position to the statement of the realization of identity with the highest aspect of the Ultimate Reality.

Abhinava's explanation

Significance of salutation

In this system, explains Abhinava, when for 'paying obeisance', the Sanskrit term *Namaskāra* or its synonyms : *Vandana, Namana, Pradhyāna* or *Jaya* (Jayati) are used, it means complete submission or surrender and dedication of the body, speech and mind exclusively to the Supreme Deity. It implies a clear consciousness of the essential superiority of the Deity (so saluted) to others. These terms imply a feeling of surrender along with the visualization of the highest power of the Supreme.

Divine grace essential

Abhinava *says* : He on whom the Supreme Grace of God is conferred can spontaneously realize the All-inclusive Universal Consciousness. Personal efforts play no part in it.[5] Abhinava had made it explicitly clear that he was explaining properly and fully *(samyak)*, the meaning of the Sūtras (i.e. the Kārikās in Utpaladeva's IP) and elucidated the Pratyabhijñā doctrine to dull-witted persons.[6] Abhinava says that his method of exposition comprises feeling of submission coupled with the visualization of the Supremacy of the highest Divinity. Hence, the word 'salutation' is not used by him in the benedictory verse form.

The Nature of causality

After explaining the position why a word denoting salutation is not included in the benedictory verse, Abhinava proceeds to explain the nature of causality. His axiom at this stage is:

"Whatever enters into consciousness is nothing but the manifestation of the Self or the Ultimate Reality."

Causality is of two types: (1) Direct and (2) Indirect.

1. *Direct causality*—that between 'means' and 'end' *(Upāya-Upeya,* cause and effect).This causality is an undeniable fact of consciousness.

2. *Indirect causality*—This causality is due to the manifestation of Māyā. It is of innumerable kinds due to the innumerable subdivisions of sentients and insentients. This is responsible for the relation between the creator and the created, the objects and means of knowledge as we find it in common life.

Supreme power as cause

The Lord, the possessor of all transcendental powers *(Anuttara-śaktiśālī)*, the essential nature of Pure Self of unlimited brilliance is also cause that cannot be intercepted by Māyā. This is of the nature of divine grace *(Anugraha-lakṣaṇa)*, the last of the five actions *(Pañca-kṛtyas)* of the highest Lord (Śiva). It helps to attain Mokṣa, the highest goal of man *(Puruṣārtha)*.

Lord's grace is another causal relation. It is of a different nature. Other causal relations are established by invariable concomitance, agreement and contrariety. Its (of the grace) essential nature is Mokṣa. The characteristic of the Supreme Creative Power is to create the impossible. It is this creative power which brings about wonderful nature. This is difficult to obtain by hundreds of wishes (expressed in an indirect manner) for the removal of the dark curtain that hides the true nature of the Ātman. Hence, the term used for it (the grace) is *Kathañcit* 'somehow' by devotion to the feet of guru who is not different from the Supreme Lord—and devotion (to whom) is inspired by the Lord Himself and had identified himself.

The above is the explanation of the term *Kathañcid* in verse (p.18).

āsādya: *Ā* in the form *'āsādya'* means 'on all sides', 'thoroughly', completely. '*Sādayitvā*' means making it unobstructedly *(nirargala)* competent for realization by his own efforts. His competence of instructing others in this *(Pratyabhijñā)* system is vindicated by his knowledge of the knowable. Otherwise he will be an imposter. The 'lyap' form *āsādya* indicates past yet (continuity of the existence) of knowledge in the present also.

Brahmā, Viṣṇu and other gods are competent but they are under the domination of lower Māyā. Partially pure souls like Mantra, Mantreśvara, Mahāmantreśvara are beyond lower Māyā but within the sphere of Mahāmāyā. There are pure souls like Sadāśiva and others, but they attained their status as Īśvara due to the power of Maheśvara. He is eternal knowledge *(Prakāśa)* and bliss *(Ānanda)*. His nature is perfect freedom. The author indicates: the great Fruit (Mokṣa) accrues from establishment of Recognition (Pratyabhijñā) with Him.

Dāsya: It expresses the competence of the devotee (here of the author); worthiness of being a recipient of Lord's will-power which is identical with Maheśvara[7].

janasya: One who is troubled constantly with births and deaths, any person (lit.one who is born). It indicates that there is no restriction on the eligibility to enter this path and one who realizes the true nature of the soul, will not suffer any reversion from self-realization. He supports his statement by quoting the *Bhagavadgītā* II.40 and *Śivadṛṣṭi* in which Somānanda, the author, states that once the omnipresence of Śiva is realized other means like scriptures etc. are superfluous.

api: (in Janasya api): Abhinava interprets it as the soul's identity with the Lord. Due to his spiritual perfection, he entertains only good of others (Abhinava expresses this in negative words: "His identity with Śiva prohibits him from entertaining any other motive than welfare of others." The commentator Bhāskara Kaṇṭha says that the word *'api'* indicates the author's identification with the person to be helped. It completely precludes the possibility of any other motive in him. Abhinava explains the word Prayojana (motive) used in his explanation quoting the definition from Nyāya System : "Prayojana is that, aiming at which man acts".[8]

icchan: This present participle of *iṣ* (*iccha)* shows that the cause of action is the object intended. And that will-power gradually develops into the power of action.

upapādayāmi: The preposition *upa* shows vicinity, nearness. It indicates bringing of men near the state of the Highest Lord. Hence the word.

samasta: in *samasta-sampad*. When one attains the state of the Highest Reality all covetable things are automatically acquired. Nothing else is left to be desired.

Abhinava quotes himself[9]: "Those who are rich in the wealth of devotion (to the Lord) have all their desires fulfilled. But for those who lack it, what is the use of coveting other things?"

Another interpretation

When the compound *samasta* etc. is expounded as attributive compound (Bahuvrīhi) the 'means' are shown : Dr. Pandey translates :

"That is the recognition of the Highest Reality *(Pratyabhijñā)* in which *(yasyām)*, clear consciousness *(samavāpti)* of the essential nature *(sampat)* of external and internal objects both existing and non-existing such as 'blue' (external objects), 'pleasure (mental i.e. internal objects) etc. *(samasta)* is the cause *(hetu)*."[10]

In Pratyabhijñā, it is taught that it is through a thorough investigation of the ultimate source of knowledge of both the internal (e.g. pleasure) and external (e.g. blue things) objects which deeply affect consciousness, the attainment of real *Paramātmā* (soul) is possible.

Abhinava quotes two verses in support:

"Merging in the self of all objective consciousness *(idam)* is its ultimate end. The consciousness that 'I am that' *(so'ham)* stands for that (Rest, *svarūpa viśrānti)*.

The term *Viśrānti* (Rest) is explained in the next verse.[11]

Ahaṁbhāva means the merging of the object in the subject. That is called rest *(viśrānti)*, perfect freedom (*svātantrya*), Supreme causal agency *(Kartṛtva)*, supreme creative power *(Īśvaratva)* as thereby all desires disappear."

This being the case, apprehension about the difficult nature of *Pratyabhijñā.* is removed. Hence, Utpala says "This path is easy and smooth."

Definition of Pratyabhijñā

'*Tasya*' means 'of Maheśvara', *Pratyabhijñā* is 'Recognition': Out of this word *jñā* is 'knowledge', *Prtīpam* 'facing oneself *(ābhimukhyena)* 'what was forgotten'. *Prtīpam* does not mean that consciousness of the *Ātman* was never a fact of experience as consciousness is ever-shining but it appears as if it is destroyed or circumscribed, through His will-power. When what was once experienced or seen is found identical with what is seen or experienced now, this unification of experiences is called 'Recognition'.[12] Thus when we had seen one person formerly, we say that this is 'Caitra'. It is recognition. *It is a cognition which refers to an object which is directly present.* [This is the difference between memory or *Smṛti* and recognition or *Pratyabhijñā. Recognition means cognition, consisting in unification of experiences at the time of the subsequent apprehension of one who was known before either in general terms or in particular* (such the son of Mr. X; of such and such description and qualities)].

The knowledge of the Lord as endowed with Supreme Power when known through Purāṇas, Āgamas or by inference and the immediate apprehension of one's own self being always there, recognition arises through the unification of the two experiences that 'I am that very Lord. I shall establish that recognition.' The last word in the verse is:

upapādayāmi— It is the first person singular of the causal form of *up* $\sqrt{pad}$-(potential-coming into existence) 'the causal form shows that the potentiality is there. I shall bring it into play through my casual agency'. The self is ever-luminous. Hence, there is the potentiality of recognition. This act simply means the removal of the influence of the obscuring Māyā. The active voice *(upapādayāmi)* shows that in bringing about recognition, there is no possibility of the agent's being affected by any purpose.

The following is the literal translation of the prose order of the verse (IP,p.18)[12A]:

> "Having somehow got union with the highest, which is the cause of the attainment of all that is attainable, and desiring the benefit of ordinary mortals by helping them in getting union with the Highest Reality, which is the means of attaining all that is attainable, through somehow bringing about His recognition, I establish His recognition which is the means of attainment of all that is attainable."
>
> —Pandey, IPV III p.7

After giving the prose order of the verse, Abhinava enters into grammatical and other subtleties and tries to show that this verse contains the gist of the whole work. Thus he says that this verse indicates: (1) subject matter *(Abhidheya)*, (2) the object *(Prayojana)*, its object *(Tat-Prayojana)*, the qualifications of the person for whom *Pratyabhijñā* system is meant, *guru-paraṁparā* or the line of preceptors *(guru-parvakrama)*, and lastly the relation *(sambandha)*.

Thus: (i) the accomplishment of the new path *(margo navo)* in 4.1.16 is the *Abhidheya* or subject matter, (ii) the object is the knowledge of the means of *Pratyabhijñā*, (iii) the object of the object is *Pratyabhijñā* itself, (iv) an ordinary mortal *(jana)* for whom the system is meant, (v) the word *Kathañcit* in the verse shows the *guru-paraṁparā* mentioned (in IP IV 2.1).

This has been stated in *Śivadṛṣṭi* by my great-grand teacher.

Thus: this verse about *Pratyabhijñā* comprises a summary of the statement of the subject matter and the author's undertaking.

Abhinava says that this work logically presents the subject in a syllogism of five terms. (IP V.I.pp.41-43) We need not go into the grammatical subtleties on practically every word of this verse and come to the beginning of the text of *Īśvara Pratyabhijñā* (IP). Even Abhinava says "enough of this subtle discussion. *(tad āstām avāntaram etat)* as the point is proved."

Conclusion of Abhinava's Introduction

Before beginning the exposition of the first verse of IP Abhinava concludes the previous introduction by stating that the object of that introductory verse is to bring about approach of the disciples to Maheśvara.

Abhinava's *Introduction to the Ist Verse*

Abhinava begins his commentary of the *Upoddhāta* with the following benedictory verse:

"It is the first creative vibration *(spanda)* of Śiva which started the manifestation of the infinite variety of objects. We always praise that Śiva."[13]

The first topic introduced is:

Proof of the existence of God

Now Īśvara is to be proved at first. But 'proof' does not mean the creation of God, as He is eternal. Those who prove the existence of God do not create Him. If it means revealing God, God Himself being of unlimited brilliance, to throw light on Him is superfluous. But what is the proof that God is self-luminous. We do not see His light in external and internal objects (for example in blue i.e. external things or pleasure, pain i.e. internal things) or in deep sleep or in unconsciousness. Granted God is self-luminous. But why is cognitive activity about him useless?[14]

To these doubts, the author (**Utpalācārya*****) replies:***

Utpala

1. *kartari jñātari svātmanyādi-siddhe maheśvare* /
   ajaḍātmāniṣedham vā siddhim vā vidadhīta kaḥ //

Translation:

Is there any sentient being who can prove or disprove the Supreme Lord (Maheśvara) who is Himself (i.e.essentially) omnipotent, omniscient, and eternal?

Abhinava: *(Summary of his commentary)*
The universe is nothing but the manifestation of the Lord who can by means of valid knowledge, advance a proof or disproof leading to the knowledge of Lord's existence or non-existence?

If *Pramātā* (Individual Soul, subject) can, is the *Pramātā* an insentient body or other than it called 'Ātman'? If (he be) insentient, an insentient body, being non-luminous, cannot throw light on others. If the *Ātman* be non-luminous, it is as good as insentient. If Ātman be self-shining, what is the essential nature of his self-luminosity? If it be merely a form of unchanging pure consciousness, it cannot differentiate cognitions or unite such differentiated cognitions by internal unification.

Hence, the Ātman must be a free self-luminous entity.

What kind of God will this self-shining entity prove or disprove. If the *Pramātā* possesses both knowledge and power, what is the difference between *Pramātā* and the *Lord*? You cannot argue that the *Pramātā* is neither omniscient or omnipotent for the term *sarva* does *not* imply any difference in the essential powers of knowledge and action.

It may be argued that objectivity of an object lies in being made to shine by the subject. We reply that what is essentially non-luminous cannot be made to shine. But if the object is of the nature of light, it sheds light in every way.

"Therefore, assuming the form known as object, the Self itself shines free from all limitations. It shines (i) to one in deep sleep (otherwise the remembrance, 'I slept soundly' will be impossible); (ii) the light is eternal as nothing limits it, and (iii) it shines to other subjects. As to difference between different *Pramātās* which is due to Prakāśa itself—it is a manifestation of Māyā." (Abhinava)[16]

Now Abhinava explains every word in the verse:

He (Maheśvara) is free

And He (Meheśvara) is free. His freedom implies power to bring out diversity in unity and unity in diversity through internal unification. The first word *kartari* in the verse represents His ultimate Omnipotential nature consisting of Bliss (*Ānanda*) and Freedom. The word *jñātari* is used to indicate that activity is essentially an offshoot of knowledge.[16A]

The words '*kartari*' and '*jñātari*' in the verse have the same import, namely 'one perfectly free to engage in all activity and is thus omnipotent'. This Freedom is the essential nature of *saṁvid* (consciousness).

Svātmani—'in his changeless nature'. This refutes the Vaiśeṣika theory of the self being insentient.

Ādisiddhe—'of limitless light or brilliance'.

Maheśvara—Being endowed with unlimited light, He manifests Himself as omniscient and omnipotent.[17]

Ajaḍātmā—Utpala refutes the insentience of Ātman as advocated by Vaiśeṣikas and Sāṅkhyas (who attribute cognition to Buddhi and not to Ātman). He asserts: An insentient self who cannot shine independently is like a stone and cannot prove or disprove anything.[18]

Abhinava concludes that discussion of the verse.

No *Ajaḍātmavādin,* believer in the sentience of the soul, can prove or disprove Maheśvara.[19] 'There is no activity of a causal agent in relation to Maheśvara, so there is neither that of the means of knowledge, because he is eternal and self-shining.

Introduction: 2nd Verse

If Maheśvara is beyond the causal agency and the means of valid knowledge, that is they cannot operate in relation to Maheśvara, what is the nature of the activity which shall help to bring about Recognition mentioned as *Pratyabhijñā*?

Utpala explains[20]

2. *kintu mohavaśādasmin dṛṣṭepyanupalakṣite* ।
śaktyāviṣkaraṇeyam pratyabhijñopadarśyate ॥

Translation:

But the powers of the self though known, are not fully realized, for these powers are concealed by the curtain, *Māyā.* But only bringing to notice these powers of the *self,* is the help to bring about the recognition of the self and nothing else.

Abhinava's Commentary

The self, being omnipotent, is absolutely free in his manifestation. He shines in forms which are wholly self-luminous or partially so. As partly self-luminous he manifests himself as *'Jīva'* or identical with them (Mantra-Maheśas), distinct from some (e.g.Vidyeśvara) or identical with some (e.g. Vijñānakala) or includes within Himself all the forms—thus these are seven forms in all.

Two extremes of these manifestations, are the lowest, *Jaḍa* (insentients) and the highest (Parama Śiva). In between are sentient beings (Jīvas). The eternally self-luminosity of Ātman is partly obscured by Lord's obscuring power called *Māyā* and all its aspects are not fully realized. At this stage, He has no causal efficiency which he possesses after complete self-realization. Lord's perfect powers of knowledge and action are to be exposed to (Jīva's) view and he is to be convinced.

The whole discussion may be summarised.[20] Thus the act of bringing about the *Pratyabhijñā* (recognition) is simply the removal of (Jīva's) ignorance. For the efficiency of the means of right knowledge—the base of practical life, consists in that much only.[20-A] For example, the verbal statement: 'This that lies in front of me is a jar, because it is directly perceived.' This verbal statement does not make the jar known, for it is already known. The verbal statement simply removes the ignorance. However, both the ignorance and its removal are simply manifestations of the Lord and nothing more.[20-A]

Introduction: Verse 3rd

We see a heap of objects of experience. It cannot be for insentients, as they have no power of knowledge. As the insentients have lost their freedom, it is impossible for them to possess the power of action, as that power owes its existence to freedom. It is not reasonable to hold that power is revealed to the insentients. If both the powers are said to refer to sentients, it will be difficult to prove that Maheśvara is the soul of all.

Utpala replies[21]

3. *tathā hi jaḍa-bhūtānām pratiṣṭhā jīvadāśrayā* I
jñānamkriyā ca bhūtānām jīvatām jīvanaṁ matam II

Translation:

The existence of the insentients depends completely on the sentients. The powers of knowledge and action are the very life of the sentients.

Abhinava explains:

'*tathā hi*' (i) Look here

(ii) *tathā* indicated *sādhya* (the proposition to be proved); *hi*—because of, on account of the reason.

Thus *tathā hi* shows that the proposition, being supported by reasons (to be stated later), is correct.

Here, as the multitudes of objects in this world are apprehended definitely, they do exist. Their existence depends on the light of consciousness. It is on the basis of determinate cognition that it (their existence) shines and it refers to the objects of experience (when the light of consciousness is shed on the objects of the world, they are existent).

A thing exists as it is determinately apprehended till it is not contradicted.[22] Substance, action and relation in their context of time and space are real, for it is in a separate definite cognition that each one of them shines.

Here Abhinava quotes: (IP II. 2.1)

> *kriyā-saṁbandha-sāmānya-dravya-dikkāla-buddhayaḥ* ।
> *satyāḥ sthairyopayogābhyām ekānekāśrayā matāḥ*[23] ॥

Translation:

The concepts of action, relation, universal, substance, place and time are not erroneous (or imaginary). They do persist because they are not proved to be false at a later stage, as in the case of appearance of two moons due to defective eyesight, and also because they have functional capacity i.e. they serve our purpose in everyday life. They are based on unity in multiplicity.

If a comprehensive view is taken, we find that though this universe is very vast it can be divided into two parts: (1) the sentients, and (2) the insentients. Out of these the insentients as objects of determinate cognition, have no independent existence. They do not possess cognitively the quality of being objective. If they possess it, they will be sentient. The insentients are essentially of the nature of consciousness but they are reduced to insentiency by the Māyā power of the Lord. They have their existence only as dependent upon the sentients and have no separate status. Only that which shines independently is really independent.

Even in the case of sentients, their bodies both gross and

subtle and vital airs are insentient and have no powers of knowledge and action. Their action is due to the sentient element in them. It is life which possesses the powers of knowing and doing. The individual subjects, have no difference in them. Hence, the individual soul must be regarded as *Īśvara* due to his powers of knowledge and actions like those of the Lord.[24]

He who has the powers of knowledge and action in a particular field is *Īśvara* to that extent of his knowledge and action, for lordliness is essentially possession of powers of knowledge and action in relation to objects. If one is not the Lord, it is against his essential nature to possess the freedom of knowledge and action. And it is the *Ātman* who knows and acts in all fields in the universe. Thus this doctrine of *Pratyabhijñā* is established.[25]

The two supra-mundane categories mentioned above viz *Sadāśiva* and *Īśvara* are merely the powers of knowledge and action. The word '*jīvatām*' used in this *Kārikā*, means 'sentient subjects'.

Introduction: Verse 4th

The powers of knowledge and action may constitute lordliness. But how do you establish that these powers are possessed by individual souls.

Utpala replies[26]

4. *tatra jñānam svataḥ siddham, kriyā kāyāśritā satī* /
parair api upalakṣyeta, tayānya-jñānam ūhyate //

Translation:

Of these, the power of knowledge as also the power of action is self-established. Power when associated with the body is perceptible by other limited perceivers. From that the presence of the powers of knowledge in others is guessed. IP 1.4

It is only on the background of self-shining self-consciousness that cognition in the past, present and future shines. This is an established fact. For if the soul is bereft of light, the whole universe would be nothing but thick darkness and not even that (i.e. would have remained non-existent). The self-luminosity of the soul will be evident even from the speech of a child. Abhinava quotes *Bṛhadāraṇyaka Upaniṣad* (II.5.19).

'Oh, by what means (of knowledge) can the knower be known.' When I say 'I know' that cognitive experience implies the consciousness of the self-luminosity of the self as well as its association with *spanda* (Supreme vibration). That it is due to this *spanda* that the sentient nature of the self as distinguished from insentient objects, is established. This *saṁrambha* or *spanda* is called *vimarśa*—the power of action. As Somānanda puts it: "When a jar etc. is cognised the subjective stir in relation to jar is action.' This internal power of action like that of knowledge is self-established and self-luminous. This internal power enters the body and being of vibrant nature exhibits itself directly as physical action in the sphere of *Māyā*. *"When such vibration (physical action) is seen in another, it leads us logically to guess the existence of the power of knowledge in him. This light of consciousness associated with the other persons is the same (as the light of consciousness in the cogniser). It means all the Pramātās (subjects/Ātmans) are One and One alone."*[27]

Abhinava substantiates his interpretation by quoting, "It is one and the same self that shines as one's own self as well as selves of others". All knowledge whether (in transcendental) *Sadāśiva* or in a worm is the knowledge of one knower. Thus the omniscience of the *Pramātā* is established.

Abhinava quotes *Śivadṛṣṭi*[28]

> "Jar (is one with myself at the time of my desire to know and therefore) knows as one with myself. And I am one with jar in knowing. *Sadāśiva* knows as myself. And I know as *Sadāśiva*. *Śiva* alone shines knowing himself through the multiplicity of objects." (Pandey)

The word *ūhyate* in the Kārikā implies that the power of knowledge is not an object of any means of right knowledge.

Thus people who realize the identity of the individual self and the universal merge everything in them. Abhinava concludes this section. This introduction (*upoddhāta*) brings out the distinctive features of the rise (*Utkarṣa*) due to *Pratyabhijñā*. This much is the purpose or the gist of the book.[29]

Abhinava gives some more explanations *of* the word *upoddhāta*.[30]

1. $\sqrt{han}$—*to know*: This is a brief presentation of the system of *Pratyabhijñā*. It removes ignorance about the content presented (*hanyate—apasāryate prameya-viṣaya-vyāmohaḥ*).

2. $\sqrt{han}$—*to go*: Going through this introduction the gist of the book is known. Paramaśiva is attained by deep contemplation of the meaning of the above four verses.

End of the chapter of *Jñānādhikāra* (Part dealing with the power of knowledge) in the *Īśvara-Pratyabhijñā-Vimarśinī* by Abhinavagupta, a disciple of the famous teacher Lakṣmaṇagupta, himself a disciple of the illustrious teacher Utpaladeva.

Introduction to Pratyabhijñā (IP IV.1)

After discussing or rather introducing the concept of *Pratyabhijñā* in the *Upoddhāta* (IP I.1.1-4), Utpala takes up the same topic in the last *Adhikāra* called *Tattvasaṅgraha.* It consists of 17 verses and the verse (No. 18 as given here) is only a concluding verse *Upasaṁhāra.* It is a concise but lucid statement of the doctrine.

In between *Jñānādhikāra* and *Tattvasaṅgraha,* we have two *Adhikāras, Kriyā* and *Āgama,* but they are polemical refutations of the objections raised by Buddhists and others against Śaivism, a response to Somānanda's criticism of the views of rival sects in his *Śivadṛṣṭi.* Utpala, being Somānanda's disciple, ably refuted the criticism of rival sects against Śaivism. But as our main topic is *Pratyabhijñā,* we shall discuss *Pratyabhijñā as stated by Utpala and as explained by Abhinavagupta.*

The following are the topics of the Kārikās in this *Adhikāra*:

(1) Maheśvara is the soul of all living beings. (v1)
(2) The real nature of bondage (v2)
(3) The essential nature of *Puruṣa* (limited soul) (v3)
(4) The essential nature of Sattva, Rajas, and Tamas (v4)
(5) Exposition of these (Sattva, Rajas, and Tamas) as qualities (*guṇa*) (v5)
(6) (Nature of) pleasure, pain, and unconsciousness or delusion (*Moha*) (v6)
(7) The object and its relation with Pati (v7)
(8) The object in relation with Paśu (limited self or subject) (v8-10)
(9) Two types of creation—general (*sādhāraṇa*) and specific (*asādhāraṇa*) (v11)
(10) Possibility of Mokṣa even though *Vikalpas* are not completely wiped out (v12)
(11) Different outlooks towards the objective world of the bound and the liberated (v13)

(12) Relation of the *Prameya* (objective world) with Parama Śiva (v14)
(13) The conclusions (points established) out of the discussion of four *Adhikāras* (v15)
(14) The line of preceptors (v16)
(15) The internal causal efficiency depends on *Pratyabhijñā* (v17)

Pratyabhijñā affords rest or peace to the causal efficiency (of knowledge and action) of *Pramātās.*

(16) *Conclusion* (v18)

Abhinavagupta's Classification of these verses (IPV II p. 280)

(1) Ultimate, real nature of (Ātman or subject)
(2-10) Nature of bondage—Real nature of *Pramātā* (subject), *Prameya* (object) and their relation
(11-17) Recognition *(Pratyabhijñā)* as the essential nature of liberation
(18) Conclusion

As in the previous section, summary of Abhinava's elucidation of every verse is included under the same verse. The heading shows the main topic of the verse.

The edition of Kashmir Sanskrit Series divides the last Adhikāra into two Āhnikas consisting of 15 and 3 verses respectively. But according to Abhinava all these verses (18) constitute one Āhnika only. I follow Abhinava.

Tattva-Saṅgraha Adhikāra

Introduction by Abhinava:
Benedictory verse[31]

ananta-māna-meyādi-vaicitryābheda-śālinam /
ātmānaṁ yaḥ prathayate bhaktānām tam stumaḥ śivam //

Abhinava's salutation:

"We eulogize that Śiva who manifests the self of devotees as possessing infinite variety of means and objects of knowledge."

In the previous three Adhikāras, it has been thoroughly proved that the Ātman in its essential nature is the same as Maheśvara (Highest Lord). This has been decided by self-experience, reason and Āgama.

For impressing the same on the minds (intellect) of pupils, a recapitulation of the contents in the 18 verses of the Āhnika is given.

Abhinava then classifies the 18 verses topic-wise (see Introduction of this Āhnika above for Abhinava's classification).

Now the meaning of the verses is explained as follows:

1. svātmaiva sarva-jantūnām eka eva maheśvaraḥ /
viśvarūpo'ham idam ityakhaṇḍāmarśa-bṛṁhitaḥ[32] //

Translation:
Maheśvara (Great Lord) alone is the soul of all living beings. He is full of unbroken consciousness that the universe is His form (He is the universe).

Abhinava explains: In this system, it is presumed that the insentients shine only as merged in the sentients. That *Idam* (consciousness of the insentients) rest on *Aham* (self-consciousness, Ī). Hence, it follows that the insentients are bereft of soul, while the living beings alone have souls. Therefore, the self and none else is Maheśvara. He is perfect. His consciousness is characterised by resting in Himself and is independent. Therefore, there is no necessity to prove His (self-evident) Omnipotence and Omniscience.

Abhinava adds:[33] There are thousands of Rudras and Kṣetrajñas who are like the sense-organs of Maheśvara in relation to the mass of objects. They belong to the Principle of Sentiency or *Cidātman.*

Objection

If the Self is the same as Maheśvara, what is that called 'bondage', from which freedom is sought?

Utpala replies:[34]

2. tatra svasṛṣṭedaṁbhāge buddhyādi grāhakātmanā /
ahaṁkāra-parāmarśa-padam nītamanena tat //

Translation:
The Lord Himself has created the objective world. He made Buddhi etc. the substratum or basis of false Ego or Self-consciousness as they are worthy of being limited subjects.

Abhinava explains: Thus Maheśvara rests within Himself. By means of His power of full-freedom, He, in the self-shining mirror of

His person, creates (shows) within Himself the objective world (*idaṁ-bhāgaḥ*) which is of a limited nature. But before doing this, He contracts Himself (*saṅkoca-puraḥ-sara*). In this creation are created objects of a dual nature. That is, they function as subjects with reference to objects not related to them. These dual-natured objects are *Buddhi, Prāṇa,* body (*Śarīra*). They are to be mentioned thus. They cannot divest themselves completely of their objective nature. So with unreal and imperfect self-consciousness, they shine (declare themselves), 'I am Caitra'. (This results in bondage.)

Objection

It may be so. But to whom is bondage applicable? Who else is there other than God?

Utpala replies:[35]

3. sa svarūpā parijñānamayo'nekaḥ pumān mataḥ ।
tatra sṛṣṭau kriyānandau bhogo duḥkhasukhātmakaḥ ॥

Translation:

It is because of the ignorance of his real self that manyness of the individual subjects is there. Such souls are many. They have individual experience of pleasure and pain. They have only limited actions (Rajas) and bliss (Sattva) (*kriyānandau*).

Abhinava explains: It is true. In reality there is no bondage whatsoever. As a matter of fact, He has the all-transcending power of freedom whereby He shows Himself to be limited. Though (even in that affected limited state) He has perfect freedom, He is not aware of it. Hence, He is called '*Puruṣa*'. *Puruṣa* signifies the ignorance of being perfect in reality. *Puruṣas* are many due to their association with different bodies, *Prāṇa* and *Buddhi*—fruit of his actions, and is in Bondage. *Bhoga* or experience of fruit is nothing but his limited action and bliss.

Abhinava explains: Limited action is suffering because Rajas is mixture of knowledge and ignorance. Its characteristic is quick activity and pain. Sattva, the light of knowledge is pleasure. Tamas is complete ignorance. It is like Pralaya.

A Query

You have used the word *sṛṣṭau* in the previous Kārikā. What is to be excluded and included therein?

The Essential Nature of Sattva, Rajas and Tamas

Utpala replies:[36]

4. svāṅga- rūpeṣu bhāveṣu patyur jñānaṁ kriyā ca yā I
māyā-tṛtīye te eva paśoḥ sattvaṁ rajas tamaḥ II

Translation:

All objects are identical with the Lord. What are called knowledge and action with reference to the objects are identical with Him. The same together with the (third power) Māyā are the three guṇas, Sattva, Rajas and Tamas of the individual.

Abhinava explains: The Lord Himself has universe as His form. So whatever consciousness and freedom there is in the universe is identical with Him. Consciousness (*Prakāśa*) and Freedom to act (*Vimarśa*) are respectively the powers of knowledge and action. Māyā is the Lord's power. It creates the discriminative consciousness of *Aham* (I) and *Idam* (This, the objective Sadāśiva and Īśvara). Their characteristic is the awareness of separate objectivity which reclines on self-consciousness. That *Prakāśa* and *Vimarśa* is the essential nature of the self is not forgotten. These three powers (*Prakāśa, Vimarśa* and *Māyā*) are natural in the Lord. They are not created. Sattva, Rajas and Tamas are characterised by pleasure, pain and delusion (*Moha*). These arise when due to the ignorance of the real nature of the soul and powers of cognition and action refer to objects supposed to be different from the soul. The consciousness is that these objects are devoid of Prakāśa and Vimarśa. The functions of these (sattva etc.) are respectively knowledge, action and restrictions (*niyamas*).

Sattva, Rajas and Tamas are Qualities

Introduction:

"If as you say, knowledge, action and *Māyā* are the inherent powers of the Lord, then *Sattva, Rajas* and *Tamas* must be non-different from *Puruṣa.* But why are they regarded different from *Puruṣa?*"

Utpala replies:[37]

5. bheda-sthiteḥ śakti-mataḥ śaktitvaṁ nāpadiśyate I
eṣāṁ guṇānām karaṇa-kāryatva-pariṇāminām II

Translation:

Practical life is based on diversity. Guṇas change into Karaṇa and Kārya (various means and objects). Hence, they should not be regarded as the powers of their possessor (viz. Pramātā).

Abhinava explains: Perfectly so (*satyam*). If there be no diversity, Guṇas would have become identical with *Pramātā*. But (in our daily life) we speak of difference between one thing and another. *Puruṣa* is only a limited sentiency. It is not his essential nature to shed light on objects. He makes them shining due to his connection to other means. *Sattva* and others are different from *Paśu* (souls) but as they help in the manifestation of external objects, they are called *guṇas*. The identity of *Puruṣa* with objects etc. would mean that *Puruṣa* has *svātantrya-śakti* (in the form of *guṇas* and it will render him *Viśvarūpa* (of universe as his form). That means that there is no *Puruṣa*. There will exist only God. Therefore, *sattva* etc. should be regarded as separate from *Puruṣa* who exist because of lack of *Pratyabhijñā*.

Pleasure, Pain and Delusion (Moha)

How do powers of *Jñāna* etc. get transformed into qualities like *sattva* etc.?

> 6. *sattānandāḥ kriyā patyus tadabhāve'pi sā paśoḥ* ।
> *dvayātmā tad-rajo duḥkhaṁ śleṣi sattva-tamomayam*[38] ॥

Translation:

Sattā (Existence, the power of being), bliss and power of action are (the powers) of the *Pati*. But *Paśus* (limited subjects) have *Sattva* and its non-being. *Rajas* which is of double nature (being and non-being) is pain. It is a compound of *Sattva* and *Tamas*.

Abhinava explains: According to this school of thought, the Lord, by His very nature is self-luminous and he protects the world after creating it. Obviously apparent variety is the characteristic of the world. The existence of Lord of the universe, His very being that is the freedom in respect of being *(Bhavana-Kartṛtā)*[39], has already been explained (in IP. I.5. 14). It is of the nature of vibration or *spanda* (flickering motion). That *sphurattā* is called the power of action. For the light of consciousness is not different from *Vimarśa*, the power of action which shines in the form of self-consciousness. It is called bliss (*Ānanda*) because it renounces dependence on others and rests in itself completely. Thus the Lord who is *Cit* (sentient) is characterised by all these powers.

In the case of *Paśu* (Pramātā or limited subject) he has both being and its absence, bliss and lack of it, as he is of limited nature. *Sattva* is that light of knowledge and pleasure in a limited subject as emanates from the Lord's power of *sattānanda* (Being and bliss). *Tamas* is the absence of *Sattā, Prakāśa* and *Ānanda* and is essentially a veil of ignorance. Just as in the feathers of a bird, two different colours(say blue and non-blue) get harmoniously mixed up, *Sattva* and *Tamas* though mutually exclusive get mixed up and shine as they can be seen together in one determinate knowledge of an object. Hence it is *Dvayātmā;* that which is mixed up in nature of Sattva and Tamas is called *Rajoguṇa.* It is of the nature of pain. Its nature of being pain (*duḥkhatva*) is due to their blend of *Sattva* and *Tamas* which are of the nature of light and darkness.

Abhinava illustrates this: Presence or consciousness of a son is dear; his absence is *Moha,* but a son with a suffering body is pain. He makes a general statement: A state free from *Sattva* and *Rajas* does not exist in the case of limited subject as such a state does not fit in any form of cognition.

Thus, there are three qualities. The word *'api'*[40] in the verse is used for *'ca'.* In the case of limited subject *'sattā'* (Being) is quality called Sattva; 'Not-being' is *Tamas.* Rajas is the mixture of the two (*dvayātmā*).

Relation between Objects and Pati

Thus far, the essential nature of *Pati* (the Lord) and *Paśu* (the limited subject) has been briefly decided. Now in order to determine the real nature of the object of perception, the relation of the objectivity (*Prameyatattva*) with the Lord is explained.

7.[41] *ye api asāmayikedantā-parāmarśa-bhuvaḥ prabhoḥ* /
te vimiśrā vibhinnāśca tathā citrāvabhāsinaḥ //

Translation:

(The objects are mere Ābhāsas.) They appear in a mixed state (*vimiśrāḥ*) or as separate from each other. But in their totality there is no internal distinction. They are the objects of the

Lord's knowledge (consciousness) of objectivity. It is expressed as 'This' but it does not indicate any conventional meaning (*a-sāmayika*).

Abhinava explains: In this school, objects are mere manifestations. Sometimes by the determinative activity different *Ābhāsas* combine into one; different *Ābhāsas* get mixed. That is the special characteristic (*Viśeṣa-rūpatā*) of the particularity. Sometimes they are regarded as non-mixed (*a-miśra*) and are universal. The term *idam* (This): the objectivity which contains the particular and universal form of objects. This consciousness is just like indicating a thing with finger.

Tathā means the objects shine variously in the same way as particular or universal. The *citratva:* the variety of forms both universal and particular (i.e. their speciality) shine simultaneously as they rest on *Ahantā* (I-ness, Principle of consciousness). Hence, it is Maheśvara who manifests this unconventional objectivity (*asāmayikīm idantām*). This being negation of subjectivity is *śūnya* (non-being).

> "The meaning of the negative particle (*Nañartha*) without reference to the negativable; which is nothing but *saṁvid* itself, but limited; and shines with the light of *saṁvid* (i.e. as identical and not different from *saṁvid*) in the state of Īśvara because it is invariably concomitant with the manifestation of the object". (Pandey[42])

Abhinava treats Kārikās 8, 9 and 10 as one unit. For the sake of easier understanding, Kārikā 8 is taken separately. Its topic is:

The object in relation with the Paśu

Introduction:

Thus far we have seen how the objective world shines to *Pati*. In the case of Lord *Parama Śiva*, even the talk of *Prameyas* (objects) does not arise. Such talks (of objects) are due to his manifestations as *Sadāśiva* and *Īśvara*. Now, Utpala describes how these *Prameyas* (subjects) shine to the limited subject, *Paśu*.

> 8. *te tu bhinnāvabhāsārthāḥ prakalpyāḥ pratyagātmanaḥ* |
> *tat tad vibhinna-sañjñābhiḥ smṛtyutprekṣādi-gocare*[43] ||

Translation:

But (*tu*) objects shine differently. They are grasped by the

Pratyagātman (individual limited self) by means of their various symbols or signs indicating words (and retained) in memory or imagination.

Abhinava explains: Tu—The word shows the difference between shining of objects to Īśvara (described above) and to *Pratyagātmans* (individual limited souls).

Bhinnāvabhāsārthāḥ etc. — the objects shine differently (in forms definite or indefinite) in memory, imagination, ideation and other types of cognition. They do so according as they are separate or mixed with other *Ābhāsas.*

It is according to the residual impressions (of Karmas) of each person. He uses his affinity or enmity indicating pleasure or pain in the previous birth that is in the case of *Pratyagātmans,* objects shine as related to different determinate cognitions, each being naturally different. Hence, their acceptance or rejection in practical life. But in the case of *Īśvara, Prameyas* are objects of pure consciousness.[44]

This is the difference between *Īśvara* and *Pratyagātman* (individual souls).

Two types of creation—general (sādhāraṇa) and specific (asādhāraṇa)

Introduction:

If the object is exactly the same irrespective of its being an object of pure consciousness and of determinate cognition what is the difference between the two viz. (i) object of the consciousness of *Īśvara,* and (ii) object determinately cognized by the limited subject (Abhinava)?

The reply is:[45]

9. *tasyāsādhāraṇī sṛṣṭir īśa-sṛṣṭy upajivanī* ।
saiṣā pyajñatayā sattyaiveśa-śaktyā tadātmanaḥ ॥
10. *sva-viśrāntyuparodhāyā calayā prāṇarūpayā* ।
vikalpa-kriyayā tattad varṇa-vaicitrya-rūpayā ॥

Translation:

The uncommon creation *(asādhāraṇi sṛṣṭi- the world of imagination* of the limited subject *(tasya) is dependent (upajīvanī)* upon the creation of the Lord *(Īśasṛṣṭi).* The limited subject is ignorant of his oneness with the Lord. Hence, it (creation of the limited subject) is not common to all limited subjects. His determinative activity is permeated by variety of letters, hence, of changing nature. This activity is due to Lord's power. Its purpose is to obstruct rest in himself.

Abhinava explains: Tasya—Creation by the limited subjects is based upon the creation of the Lord. As it depends on the creation of the Lord, it is not common and is related to particular subject (its creator and not common to other subjects). What may be pleasant to the creating person is not so to others. If the limited subject has the power of creating (common objects), then he will be God himself. Yes, he is the Lord himself but he does not know his (God-like) power and therefore his creation is not common to other subjects and in other times, as is the case with Lord's creation. The Lord is responsible for emergence of the power of grasping determinately.

God being a repository of all ideas is characterised by a mass of words (*śabdarāśi*). The function of that power is to conceal the Lord's state of being at rest with himself. This power is the eight groups of letter (like *k, kh,* etc.) presided over by deities like Brāhmī, etc.

[Words consist of letters of alphabet. These are presided over by deities like Brāhmī. These deities conceal Lord's pristine state.] The uncommon creation of the individual is of varied arrangement of letters e.g. 'This is a friend or an enemy'. The subject is essentially identical with the Lord. So the creation of his imagination, for example, 'An elephant with five trunks and four tusks runs in the sky' is a creation of determinative cognitive power. It is a peculiar unification of *Ābhāsas.*

Thus all that is created by a limited subject in the field of determinate cognition is based upon the creation of the Lord.

According to Abhinava's introduction to this *Adhikāra* vv11-17 deal with the doctrine of *Pratyabhijñā.*

Abhinava in continuation of v10 raises the question: If this creation by *Paśus* (limited subjects) is only phenomenal, what will the creation of the Lord do to the *Paśu*?

Utpala gives the decision.[46]

> *11. sādhāraṇo 'nyathā caiṣaḥ sargaḥ spaṣṭāvabhāsanāt* I
> *vikalpa-hānenaikāgryāt krameṇa īśvaratāpadam* II

Translation:

The creation (sarga) is of two types: (i) common (*sādhāraṇa*) and (ii) the other is uncommon (*anyathā*) for both of them are clearly manifest (*spaṣṭāvabhāsanāt*). The state of *Īśvara* is gradually attained by giving up the determinative activity (*Vikalpa-hānena*) and concentrating (that I am this i.e. *Īśvara*) (*aikāgryāt*). *Abhinava explains:* The creation of the Lord is of two types: (i) common e.g. a jar etc. and (ii) uncommon (*anyathā*). The word '*anyathā*' means (sight of two moons as mentioned before). The common characteristic of these creations is their clear manifestation (*spaṣṭāvabhāsana*). If a clearly manifest object that is grasped only indeterminately, is concentrated upon through a gradual process of giving up determinancy, this creation is referred to 'I am this' as in the experience at the level of Īśvara (*aiśvarya-parāmarśapada*). Then as a result of the practice of *Śāṁbhavī Mudrā*,[47] the concentration slowly destroys the *Paśutva* (the nature of a limited subject) of a *Paśu* (individual soul or subject) and makes the nature of Īśvara (*Īśvaratva*) manifest.

If this *Vikalpa-sarga* (creation of determinative activity of limited subject called *pāśava*) be *anyathā* (otherwise, that is if the creation of the determinative activity be of one who has realised his identity with the power of the Lord), then that creation is common. It is so like the creation of one who has realized the Lord, his mind thoroughly absorbed (in the idea represented by a Mantra) and applies his *mantra* for reconstruction of health, bringing about death, or for pacification[48].

Attainment of Mokṣa despite residual Vikalpas

Introduction:

Mokṣa (liberation) is nothing but self-realization which is nothing but the realization of Parama Śiva. This is attained when through complete shedding of *Viklapas,* one identifies oneself with what is free from determinancy. The author, Utpala, shows the possibility of attainment of *Mokṣa* despite residual *Vikalpas.*

> *12. sarvo mamāyaṁ vibhava ityevaṁ parijānataḥ*[49] |
> *viśvātmāno vikalpānāṁ prasare 'pi maheśatā* ||

Translation:

One (individual soul) who knows thoroughly (*pari-jānataḥ*) that all this majesty is his and he himself is the universe, attains Īśvarahood even when *vikalpas* (determinate cognition) are still spreading.

The individual soul which is called *Paśu* and is not other than I, is not different from God. He is the light of consciousness. He grasps both subject and object. That transcendental being is no other than I. Hence, the creation of *vikalpas* is a characteristic of my freedom. When this conviction is firmly rooted, the subject, though his *Vikalpas* are not completely wiped out, becomes liberated even in this life-time. This is certainly a state of freedom from doubt. In this even doubt is not doubted.

Difference of outlook in the liberated and in one bound

If that be the case, what is the difference between a subject (individual soul) in bondage and one who is liberated?

Utpala replies'[50]

13. meyam sādhāraṇaṁ muktaḥ svātmābhedena manyate /
maheśvaro yathā baddhaḥ punaratyantabheda-vat //

Translation:

Like the great Lord, the liberated soul regards all measurable and discernable objects as non-different from himself, while a soul in bondage regards (all objects) as totally different from him.

The liberated regards himself to be identical with that I-consciousness which is the ruler or protector of all (individual souls) beginning from Lords *Sadāśiva, Īśvara* to worms. He thinks that all objects of cognition of all beings in the universe are mine. Similarly all objects of my cognition are those of all beings in the universe. He regards the objects as part of himself. He gradually realizes that all objects (*Prameyas*) are not different from one another and from himself. Finally everything is merged into complete unity.

But in the case of the bound, everything is opposite to this as his basis is on pure diversity.

Relation between the objective world and Śiva

Thus far we have considered how objects appear at the stages of *Sadāśiva* and *Īśvara*. We have seen them in relation to the liberated and the *Paśu* (limited subject).

How does the object stand in relation to Parama Śiva?

Utpala replies:[51]

14. sarvathā tvantarālīnānanta-tattvaugha-nirbharaḥ /
śivaḥ cidānanda-ghanaḥ paramākṣara-vigrahaḥ //

Translation:

In Śiva a flood (mass) of infinite Tattvas is completely merged. They rest in Him (in the form of saṁvid). He is *Cit* (consciousness) and *Ānanda* (bliss) incarnate. His person (*vigraha*) is supremely imperishable and changeless. (Thus the problem of *Prameyas*, objects of knowledge does not arise at all.)

Abhinava explains: In the case of the highest Lord Śiva the problem of the relation of objects of knowledge does not exist. For the flood or mass of Tattvas completely merge in Him as it rests on pure *cit (cid-rūpatā-mātra-viśrāntatvād)*. That state is of the nature of *saṁvid* which is characterised by rest on self, the *Ānanda* (Bliss) which is only spontaneous nature of self-consciousness (*Saṁvit-svabhāva*). It is absolutely changeless self-consciousness. It is the transcendental state of the Lord who is the universe. There is no break in his transcendental greatness. He being eternally pure, the talk of object does not arise. It is described as all-transcendent.

Résumé of all the four Adhikāras[52]

15. evam ātmānam etasya samyag-jñāna-kriye tathā /
jānan yathepsitān paśyan jānāti ca karoti ca //

Translation:

Thus having fully and adequately realized the soul (*Ātman*) with all its powers of knowledge and action and having fully understood that the powers are non-different from the soul, he knows and does anything as per his desire.

Abhinava explains: In this way, He knows that the soul (self) is the veritable *Īśvara* Himself and His powers of knowledge and action are the same as the power of freedom and are non-different from Him. The subject who realizes that powers of knowledge and action are the same as those of the Lord and engages himself in the practice of *Samāveśa*, attains the capacity to know and do whatever he desires while he is alive. But he who does not practice *Samāveśa* is liberated while alive and merges in the supreme Lord after death.

The Line of Preceptors

For establishing the truth or reliability of a proposition, three *pracītis* (investigations or examinations) are prescribed: (1) It must be the experience of the person concerned (*Ātma-pracīti*), (2) It must be supported by the line of preceptors (*Guru-pracīti*); and (3) *Śāstra-pracīti*—It must be based on or substantiated by Śāstra or Āgama.

This teaching is a part of the personal experience of the author, yet the teaching of the line of preceptors has corroborated it. In the Adhikāra called *Āgama,* the support of Śāstra is shown. This (teaching) is confirmed by the line of preceptors, by (Āgama), Śāstra and by personal experience.

With this aim in view, he states his preceptorial line:

> 16. *iti prakaṭito mayā sughaṭa eṣa mārgo navo*
> *mahāgurubhir ucyate sma śivadṛṣṭi-śāstre yathā* ǀ
> *tadatra nidadhat padam bhuvana-kartṛtām ātmano*
> *vibhāvya śivatāmayīm aniśam āviśan siddhyati*[53] ǀǀ

Translation:

Thus this new easy way (to Mokṣa) has been made open (to the public) by me. It is as it was spoken (explained) in the Śiva-Dṛṣṭi Śāstra by my great preceptor (Somānandācārya). Therefore, a person who thus treads this path and realizes that he is the maker (creator) of the universe, He becomes a Siddha after his complete merger in (Lit. enters into complete identity with) Śivahood.

Abhinava explains: I have made public this new and easy (*sughaṭa*) path to *Mokṣa.* It is easy as it does not involve external (such as sacrifices, performance of rituals—Bhāskara Kaṇṭha) and internal discipline such as breath-control and other yogic procedures) which involves troubles.

It is 'new' in the sense that it was not publicly known, as it remained concealed in scriptural texts. It is promulgated by my great preceptor in his work *Śivadṛṣṭi-śāstra.* While doing this, he refuted the objection of rival schools. This matter is substantiated by scriptures, (line of) teachers and personal experience. Therefore, (*Tad*) when a person follows this path with concentration and realizes his omnipotence, he becomes firmly convinced. He thereby gets liberated while in this birth and becomes one with Śiva.

As has been said by the revered great-grand-preceptor: "When the omnipresence of Śiva's essential nature is realized through definite personal experience, there remains no propriety of means of valid knowledge and concentration. When actual gold is directly known, contemplation as the means of its knowledge becomes superfluous. Just as it is undisputed that we have parents etc. that knowledge is equally firm and valid."

After realization of one's identity with Śiva, if one remains merged in Him along with his body, mind and śūnya, one attains all spiritual powers (*vibhūtis*) upto the highest one.

Fruit of Pratyabhijñā

Causal efficiency (of knowledge and action) of Pramātās due to Pratyabhijñā

From what you say, if the essential nature of the 'thing' called Ātman be (eternally) the same in its causal efficiency, there will be no difference irrespective of *Pratyabhijñā* (Recognition) or non-recognition. You sow seed and it sprouts up, whether you recognize it or not.

Abhinava explains the difference: There are two types of causal efficiency (*arthakriyā*): (1) External: sprouting forth of seeds, and (2) Internal: feeling of pleasure which is essentially self-consciousness, the rest of the subject (Pramātṛ) in himself. The first requires no *Pratyabhijñā* (Recognition). It is for the second that *Pratyabhijñā* is necessary. For here the consciousness that 'I am Maheśvara' must be awakened. This consciousness confers both higher and lower *siddhis* and glories of being liberated during the life-time of the Pramātṛ. Utpala gives an illustration (*Dṛṣṭānta*) to show that causal efficiency which is essential rest on the soul (*Pramātṛ-viśrānti-sārārtha-kriyā*) is not seen without *Pratyabhijñā* and is experienced instantly with *Pratyabhijñā*.

Now a romantic illustration in a work of serious philosophy.

Utpala tells:

Effectiveness of Pratyabhijñā (Recognition)

17. *taistair api upayācitair upanatas tanvyās sthito' pyantike*
kānto loka-samāna evam aparijñāto na rantuṃ yathā /
lokasyaiṣa tathānavekṣitaguṇaḥ svātmāpi viśveśvaro
naivālam nija-vaibhavāya tadiyaṁ tat pratyabhijñoditā[54] //

Instead of Abhinava's exposition, the following episode described in the verse will be interesting.

A certain young lady fell in love with a young man (the hero) by hearing many of his excellent qualities. She had an intense desire to see him. She sent letters and messengers to him describing how she was getting emaciated by the pangs of separation from him.

In response to her urgent messages, the hero came to see her. But she could not discern any of his excellences and thought him to be an ordinary man.

Abhinava here philosophically remarks : Under such circumstances the perception of the object, though it actually takes place, does not give any satisfaction to the heart. Similarly, though the Lord of universe is ever shining within us, as the very Self, yet His light does not fill the heart with bliss (*Ānanda*) because the self is not realized. The self, therefore, shines as an ordinary object like 'jar' (Pandey).

The story continued: But when she cognised those excellences through her messenger—friend (*guru*—in this case) her heart immediately bloomed forth and in consequence of repeated enjoyment of union, she experiences the rest of the heart.'

Now Abhinava philosophizes: When transcendental lordliness is recognized in the self as a result of guru's enlightenment, then immediately in this very life, one gets liberation characterized by perfection. If one makes repeated efforts for merging in the Supreme, he gets spiritual powers.

Thus, it is the recognition of the self which gives higher and lower spiritual powers. Abhinava adds: This system which gives final liberation is beneficial to all.

Utpala concludes:[55]

> 18. *janasyāyatna-siddhyartham udayākara-sūnunā* I
> *īśvara-pratyabhijñeyam utpalenopapāditā* II

Translation

For the sake of effortless or easy attainment of *siddhi* (transcendental power or liberation) by an ordinary person, Utpala, the son of Udayākara has written this *Īśvara-Pratyabhijñā*.

Abhinava concludes his Bhāṣya as follows.[56] After affirming that the meaning of Utpala's Kārikās are so clearly explained that nobody can adversally criticise them: He says that it is on his personal experience that the system is based in which Mīmāṁsā, Nyāya, Vyākaraṇa and Śaiva Āgamas became helpful for self-realization. He confidently says: "Only the sun and nobody else can unite the juices of earth and water for the growth of food-grains. The realization of the self is a pre-condition for discussing the Śāstras. "Others are ineligible," concludes Abhinava with reference to the critics.

The usual colophon : *The commentary called Vimarśinī Tattva-saṅgrahādhikāra of Utpaladeva's Īśvara-Pratyabhijñā is completed.*

Chapter 4

Kṣemarāja on *Pratyabhijñā* Philosophy

Introduction

As we have seen before, Kṣemarāja, an eminent disciple of Abhinavagupta, was an authoritative writer on *Īśvarādvayavāda,* popularly known as Kashmir Śaivism. He wrote lucid commentaries on Tantras like the *Svacchanda* and *Netra.* Apart from his authoritative commentary on Vasugupta's *Śivasūtra,* he wrote two commentaries on Vasugupta's *Spanda Kārikā. Spanda-sandoha* was on its first Kārikā in which he deals with the entire Spanda system. His *Spandanirṇaya* is a commentary on the entire *Spanda Kārikā.* His commentaries on Utpala's *Stotrāvali* and *Krama Sūtra* are well-known. His commentary on Abhinavagupta's *Locana* (a commentary on *Dhvanyāloka*) shows his mastery over Poetics.

Thus Kṣemarāja was a versatile writer who wrote on Poetics, Tantra and Śaiva Philosophy. The most important philosophical work contributed by Kṣema (rāja) is *Pratyabhijñā Hṛdaya* 'The heart, i.e., the essence of the doctrine of *Pratyabhijñā* (Recognition)'. As I stated before, next to Abhinavagupta, Kṣemarāja is an authority on Monistic Śaivism in general and Pratyabhijñāśāstra in particular.

The Aim

The aim of Kṣema (rāja) is to elucidate the main tenets of the *Pratyabhijñā* system lucidly and succinctly. In the very first paragraph of the book, he states:

"The truth of the teaching of *Pratyabhijñā* is explained briefly for those devoted people who aspire after *Samāveśa* (getting merged in the Lord), but who have not studied different work on Logic or Dialectics and hence have not developed intellectual capacity to understand or grasp the *Pratyabhijñā*. In other words, it is for a devoted layman whom Kṣema addresses.[1] Naturally, he avoids polemics. On the other hand, Kṣema's teacher Abhinava formally states that in order to elucidate the concept of Recognition (*Pratyabhijñā*) to people of slow understanding, he explains the contents of the work of Utpaladeva called *Īśvara-pratyabhijñā*.[2] He expresses his wish: May this (Abhi's) exposition be helpful to all people of slow understanding[3]. But Abhi's commentary is a bit tough and full of polemics. His very Introduction (pp. 17-47) and the refutation of the objections of the Buddhists and of other schools of Philosophy against Śaivism in the *Jñāna* and other *Adhikāras* (Chapters) is a proof of his scholarship and proficiency in dialectics. The final verse of his commentary implies that nobody who has not realised the self is eligible to question him regarding Śāstric discussion.[4] This is a bit over-confidence.

Compared with his teacher Abhinava, Kṣema appears to be rather modest. In addition to his desire to explain the *Pratyabhijñā* to the lay public, he feels that his attempt to bring out the quint-essence of *Pratyabhijñā* which is a *Śāṅkaropaniṣad*, will nullify the poison of Saṁsāra."[5]

The Aim of this Work

Pratyabhijñā is the recognition of one's identity with Lord Śiva. This is attainable by easy means and its consequent great fruit *(Mokṣa)* as well. The exposition is given with this aim in view.[6] As the work deals with the recognition of *Cit*, we should know the nature of *Cit*.

What is *Cit*?

Our individual soul may be Parama Śiva or *Cit*. But what is *Cit*? Here in the text the form *Citi* is used. The Highest Power is both He or She or neither. It is used in the singular number as it is not limited by Time, Space, Form, etc. *Citi* is the Ultimate Reality, *Parā Saṁvit*. It is *prakāśa-vimarśa-maya*. The words *prakāśa* and *vimarśa* cannot be adequately translated into English. *Parā-saṁvit*, 'supreme consciousness', is a non-relational, changeless principle. It is a coalescence into undivided unity of *Aham* (the individual soul) and *Idam* (the outside universe). *Prakāśa* means 'light', but it is self-luminous as well as illuminating others. If *Cit* were only *prakāśa* without vimarśa, it would have lost its status as 'Maheśvara' and as consciousness. It would have become inert like a jar.[7] Just as the sun is self-luminous though there be nothing to illuminate, this *Prakāśa* is not dependent on the objects to be illuminated.[8]

Vimarśa: Grammatically the term is derived from *vi-*$\sqrt{}$*Śmṛś* (to grasp with intellect). But in this (*Trika*) Śāstra, it means non-relational, immediate awareness (*visphuraṇa*) of 'I'. It has the power to create etc. the universe as Kṣema puts it in *Parāprāveśikā*.[9] It is *cid-rūpiṇī śakti*. Hence, *vimarśa* is called differently as *parā śakti, parā vāk, svātantrya, sphurattā, sāra, hṛdaya*. It is a *Visphuraṇa*. Without *vimarśa* Śiva will be *Jaḍa*.[10]

This Ultimate Reality *citi* is both universal consciousness and universal psychic power. This all-inclusive universal consciousness is called *Anuttara*—that beyond which there is nothing higher. It is the highest Reality. It is the changeless Principle of all manifestation.

Preview of the work

As the work is a systematic exposition of *Citi* in twenty Sūtras, a preview of the Sūtras will give a succinct idea of the work.

The following are the topics of the Sūtras:

(1) *Citi* (consciousness) is absolutely free. By its own free will, it causes the manifestation, maintenance and withdrawal of the universe.

(2) By dint of the power of her Free Will, she displays the universe upon her own back.

(3) Analytical exposition : Variety (*nānātva*) in the universe due to the differentiation of the reciprocally adapted subject and object.

(4) Every individual soul (*pramātā*) is Śiva (in a contracted form).

(5) *Citta* (individual consciousness) is a contraction of *Citi* (universal consciousness) after descending from its *Cetana* stage.

(6) *Citta:* the real form of *Māyā pramātā* (who is only *citta*)

(7) The multifarious nature of the soul.

(8) The fundamentals of various systems of philosophy are the different roles of the Ātman.

(9) How the Ātman is covered with *Mala*.
(10) The soul (in the restricted condition) performs the five functions of *Śiva*.
(11) Esoteric *Pañca-krytas* (five functions) of a *Yogin*.
(12) What is *saṁsāritva* (state of being involved in saṁsāra).
(13) *Citta* becomes *Citi* by acquiring the knowledge of the *pañca-kṛtyas* (five functions of the self) and rising to the status of *Cetana*.
(14) The fire of *Citi* though covered with Māyā in a descended state, partly burns the fuel of *karmas* (or known objects)
(15) By the re-emergence of its (inherent) power it makes the universe its own.
(16) The steady experience of identity with *Cit* means *jīvan-mukti* (liberation during lifetime).
(17) By the development of the centre, the bliss of the spirit is acquired.
(18) Means for the development of the centre.
(19) Permanent *samādhi* is attained by dwelling on one's identity with *Cit* (universal consciousness).
(20) After attainment of *krama-mudrā* and entrance into perfect I-consciousness—an essence of consciousness and bliss—of the nature of mantra power, one attains lordship over the deities of consciousness which bring about all emanation and re-absorption of the universe.

All this is the nature of the soul.

As *Pratyabhijñā* is the 'recognition of the highest principle', the nature or the characteristic of that principle called *citi* needs elucidation. Hence, in the very first Sūtra, Kṣema, gives its two main characteristics, namely freedom and creatorship of the universe.[11] The term 'freedom' (*svātantrya*) in Trika Philosophy is so comprehensive that all powers attributable to self or Śiva are addressed to it.[12] It is due to the importance of the concept of Freedom that the system is designated as '*svātantryavāda*'. It is also *spanda* (vibration)which appears to sparkle though steady.[13]

The comprehensiveness of the term will be evident from its various synonyms each representing its particular aspect. They are: *caitanya, sphurattā, spanda, sattā, mahāsattā,* the ability to create the world and freedom in all activities.[14]

Sūtra 1: Nature of Citi

1. *citiḥ svatantrā viśva-siddhi-hetuḥ*[11] ǀ

Translation:

Citi is absolutely free. She is the cause of the creation of the universe.

Kṣema explains (summary): "*Citi* (the universal consciousness) brings about the creation (*sṛṣṭi*), maintenance (*sthiti*) and withdrawal (*saṁhāra*) of the universe consisting of all Principles (*Tattvas*) from *Sadāśiva* to the earth. (See *Supra* p23—Introduction—the universe, *viśva*). It is thus the *hetu* or cause of the universe. She consists of *vimarśa* power. She is the absolute 'free will' who does not require any external help (*upādāna*) for creation etc. She can do anything by sheer free will-power. She is non-different from Śiva. It is the light of this consciousness which causes (the creation, maintenance and withdrawal of) the universe. No other entity like *Māyā*, *Prakṛti* etc. can do it. *Citi* vitalized Time, Space, and Form. They cannot penetrate her, as she is all-pervading, eternally risen (*nityodita*) and perfectly satisfied in herself"[15]

After succinctly explaining the sūtra, he replied some objections to this concept:

If everything is *Cit*, the universe must be non-different from *Cit*. In a causal relation cause and effect are different. How can *Citi* be *hetu* (cause) of the universe which is identical with it?

Reply: *Pramāṇas* (means of valid knowledge like perception) cannot be applied to *Citi*. She is absolute, free-willed. She flashes forth in the form of innumerable worlds.

Another Interpretation

Citi is the cause of the *siddhi* (creation) as well as *saṁhāra* (the *sāmarasya* or identity with the highest non-dual consciousness). Hence, she is free-willed and is the cause of *siddhi* (enjoyment in this world (*bhoga*) and liberation from *Saṁsāra* (*mokṣa*).

Kṣema's Notes:

(1) *Citi*—Its singular number shows that she is not limited by Space, Time, Form and denies duality.

(2) *Svatantrā* (absolute Free Will): The supreme power is the essence of *Cit* and is distinguished from (Śaṅkara's

concept of) Brahman which requires help of *avidyā* for creation.

(3) *Viśva* etc.: *Cit* is omnipotent, the cause of everything, an easy path to *Mokṣa* and the great fruit (*Mokṣa*).

Sūtra 2: Display of the Universe

Objection: If *Citi* be the cause or creator of the universe, she must be in need of some material, instruments, etc. If *Citi* be different from the material cause, it amounts to the acceptance of Dualism.

Sūtrakāra replies[16]

2. *svecchayā sva-bhittau viśvam unmīlayati* /

Translation:

It is by the power of her Will (and not with any other outside material or upādāna) that she displays (unfolds - *unmīlayati*) upon her own (screen-like) background (*sva-bhittau*).[16]

Kṣema explains: the following terms in the Sūtra:

(1) *svecchayā:* By her own Free Will. *Citi* does not require the help of *Avidyā* as in *Vedāntic Brahmavāda*. Just as she has independent will-power, she has no necessity of any external *upādāna* for the creation (etc.) of the world. If this characteristic of Free Will is denied, *Citi* ceases to be *cit*. There is no difference in *Citi* and free-will. Hence, this doctrine is known also as *svātantrya-vāda* (the doctrine of Freedom).

(2) *svabhittau*: On the (screen-like) back i.e. within herself, as there is no space outside *Citi*. Just as a city reflected in the mirror appears different from the mirror, here the universe though non-different from her appears as different.

(3) *unmīlayati:* The universe is within *Citi*, lying dormant. *Citi* displays it by making it appear on herself.

Kṣema concludes: The universe—its existence in *Citi*, is identical with *Citi's* light.[17]

Sūtra 3: Analytical exposition: variety (nānātva) nature of the universe.

In order to clarify the nature of the universe the 3rd Sūtra states:

3. *tan nānā anurūpa grāhya grāhaka-bhedāt*[18] /

Translation:

The universe is manifold (nānā). The reason—there is differentiation (*bhedāt*) of reciprocally adapted (*anurūpa*) objects (*grāhya*) and subject (*grāhaka*).

Kṣema at first gives the meaning of every word in the *Sūtra* as follows:

tat—the universe
nānā—manifold
anurūpa—the state of reciprocal adaptation
bheda—differentiation

Kṣema states the reciprocal adaptation of object and subject at different stages as follows:[19]

(1) In the principle called *Sadāśiva* (3rd in the hierarchy from Śiva) there is the experience that the total universe (*viśva*) is an object *(grāhya)* and is both identical and different. In this stage, the experience is: 'I am this'. Here 'I'ness *(ahantā)* dominates the experience of the universe—'this-ness' (*idantā*) is not explicit (*asphuṭa*). The *pramātṛs* (experient, souls) in this stage are called *Mantra-Maheśvaras.* They are goverened by *Sadāśiva.* The comparative table given at the end of this section will show how the *Idantā* factor becomes progressively predominant so much so that ultimately *idantā* (consciousness of external universe) becomes completely predominant. The widening gap between the consciousness of *ahantā* (I-ness, subject aspect) and *idantā* (This-ness, the objective) world may briefly be summarised thus:

(2) *Īśvara* (the fourth principle): At this stage, the universe is apprehended in the form 'I am this': consciousness of 'I' (*ahantā*) and that of the universe (*idantā*) are *sphuṭa* (distinct) simultaneously. The consciousness of individuals called Mantreśvara is of this type. These individuals are governed by Īśvara.

(3) *Vidyā* or Śuddha vidyā: Individual souls in this stage are called *Mantras.* They have a balanced consciousness of 'I'ness and 'This'-ness (*idam,* the world). There are many distinctions among them.

(4) In a stage above Māyā and below Śuddha Māyā[20], the individual souls are called *vijñānakalas.* They are of the nature of pure consciousness *(śuddha-bodhātmānaḥ)* but have no power of action.

(5) *Māyā*: Individual souls at this stage are *pralaya-kevalins* or *śūnya*. Their field of experience is the insensible, that is they do not have clear consciousness, of *ahaṁ* and *idam*. This is quite suitable to their stage.

(6) After the *pralayākalas* are *sakalas* (from Māyā to the principle Earth). They are different from everything else. Their field of experience is limited and different as themselves (*tathābhūtam*). Though there is such a variety, actually it is the Parama Śiva (the Highest Lord Śiva) alone who manifests Himself in numerous multiplicity. There is no *grāhya* (object) or *grāhaka* (subject).[21]

To sum up: Multiplicity (*nānātva*) emerged as following stages or tattvas:

The Principle	*Presiding Deity*	*Pramātā Experient Soul*	*Field of Consciousness*
1. Śiva	Śiva	Śiva Pramātā	Everything is Śiva (*Aham-vimarśa*).
2. Sadāśiva	Sadāśiva	Mantra-Maheśvara	Dominant *I-ness* Faint consciousness of the world.
3. Īśvara	Īśvara	Mantreśvara	More consciousness about the world (*idam*).
4. Śuddha vidyā	Ananta	Mantra	Balanced consciousness of *aham* and *idam*.
5. Mahāmāyā	—	*Vijñānakala**	*Pralayākala**and *sakala**
6. Māyā Tattva	—	*Pralayakala* or śūnya pramātā	Śūnya
7. Remaining Tattvas upto Pṛthvī, the last Tattva	—	*Sakala**	Differences in all objects.

**Paśus* i.e limited subjects or individual bound souls are classified as follows:

(1) *Sakala*—A *paśu* bound with *āṇava, kārma* and *māyīya* mala.

(2) *pralayākala*—A *paśu* bound with *āṇava* and *kārma* malas, as *māya* vanishes at the time of *pralaya*.

(3) *vijñānakala*—A *paśu* with āṇava mala only. By observing penance, *vratas*, this goes on decreasing. Finally with the grace of Śiva, *paśu* regains his original Śivahood.

Sūtra 4: Every pramātā (individual soul) is Śiva (in a contracted form)

4. *citi saṅkocātmā cetano'pi saṅkucitaviśvamayaḥ* I

If Lord Śiva has the whole of the universe as His body (viśva-śarīra), the *cetana* (pramātā or individual soul) in whom *citi* or consciousness is in a contracted form, must have the universe as his body in a contracted form.[22] Pramātā (the individual soul, grāhaka or subject) is identical with Śiva who has the universe as His body (*viśva-śarīra*). His true nature is light of consciousness. It is due to Śiva's *Māyā-śakti* that the *pramātā* (individual soul) appears contracted. But contraction is of the *cit* or consciousness only. Every *pramātā* is identical with Śiva whose body is the universe. That is the position in a nutshell.

Now let us follow Kṣema's elucidation of the Sūtra.

The universe is within Śiva. When he desires to manifest it in the form of Sadāśiva and in other suitable forms, He flashes forth at first as non-different from the light of consciousness but He does not experience the unity of consciousness wherein the universe is identical with consciousness (*cidaikya-akhyāti-maya*).[23]

[In this state Śiva is called *anāśrita*. Śiva is not related to anything or has no objective content. This state is intermediate between Śakti Tattva and Sadāśiva Tattva. In this state, Śakti begins to isolate the universe from the self by producing ignorance (*ākhyāti*) about his nature. The self forgets his identity (I-ness) with the universe. This loss of experience is Saṁsāra.]

As this stage is not related to anything or has no objective content, He is called *anāśrita Śiva.*[23] From the point of view of objective manifestation, He is *Śūnya.*

Then He flashes forth in principles, worlds (*bhuvanas*), entities or objects (*bhāvas*) and their respective Pramātās. These are crystalized forms (*āśyā natārūpa*) of the *Cit* essence.

Just as Śiva is universe-bodied (viśva-rūpa), the individual soul's body has the whole universe contracted within him like a banyan tree lying in a concentrated form in its tiny seed.

Here Kṣema quotes some Āgamic authorities. They say: "Experient or individual soul is identical with Śiva whose body is the universe. Due to Śiva's Māyā Śakti, *pramātā's* (individual soul's) real nature is not manifested. The contraction is of *Cit* (consciousness) only." Kṣema quotes his own verse: "If akhyāti or nescience is that which is never experienced, then knowledge (*khyāti*) remains. If *akhyāti* (ignorance) be experienced, it becomes of the nature of *Khyāti* that is only *Khyāti* remains." He further quotes *Spanda Kārikā* which says: "Jīva is identical with the whole universe and Śiva is present in every stage (whether in the word or object or in its mental grasp). In this way the non-difference between *Jīva* and *Śiva* is stated. The knowledge of this real position constitutes *mukti* (Liberation) and ignorance about this bondage."[25]

Sūtra 5: Citta (Individual consciousness) is a contraction of Citi (universal consciousness)

The doubt raised: The previous Sūtra has shown non-difference between Śiva and the individual soul (pramātā, grāhaka or Subject). But the individual soul (*grāhaka*) is by nature full of *vikalpas* (differentiation activity). This activity is due to *Citta* (individual consciousness). That being the nature of *Citta*, how can the individual be of the nature of Śiva (Śivātmakatva)?

Kṣema replies:[26]

citireva cetanapadādavarūḍhā
cetya-saṅkocinī cittam /

Translation:

It is (none else but) *Citi* which comes down from the stage called Cetana (complete uncontracted consciousness). As it gets contracted it becomes *Citta* (individual consciousness). Its contraction is in conformity with the objects of consciousness (cetya).

Kṣema explains: As a matter of fact, *Citta* (individual consciousness) is the supreme *Citi*.[27] It is *Citi*, who of her own accord comes down from the stages of *Cetana*. If the predominance of *Cit* is acquired through Yogic practices like *samādhi*, the *śuddha-pramātā* (i.e. follower of śuddhādhvā) gradually progresses through stages like Īśvara, Sadāśiva and reaches the highest stage.

To sum up:

Citi comes down from its state of *Cetana*. She is then disposed to comprehend external objects of consciousness (such as a blue object) and internal objects of consciousness (such as pleasure, pain) and thus becomes *Citta*. Kṣema quotes here *Īśvara-Pratyabhijñā*[28] (IV. 1-4.). It states the correspondence of the powers of the Lord and *guṇas* of *Paśu*.

Powers of the Lord	*Paśu's guṇas*
Jñāna	Sattva
Kriyā	Rajas
Māyā	Tamas

Citi has the above powers, but owing to limitations, in the *paśu* stage, the powers become qualities such as Sattva etc.

The individual consciousness, despite *vikalpas* is of the nature of Śiva— the self-luminous character of the inmost nature never disappears. Thus a common man need not underestimate himself.

Sūtra 6 Citta: The real form of māyā-pramātā

Citta (individual consciousness) may be of the nature of Śiva ultimately, but its real nature is *māyā-pramātā* i.e. the individual soul, the experience of the impure path (*aśuddhādhvan*). It includes *pralayākala* and *Sakala* souls.

The Sūtra states:

6. *tan-mayo māyā pramātā*[29] ।

Translation:

The Māyā-Pramātā is comprised of *Citta*.

Kṣema explains: In the sphere of body and soul, *Citta* alone is predominant. The sphere of *Śūnya* (void) is also comprised of the impressions (*saṁskāras*) of *Citta*, otherwise one would not remember anything after sleep.

Vasugupta says that the soul is universal consciousness (*caitanya*), but while discussing the characteristics of *Māyā-Pramātā* he says, "individual consciousness" is the soul.[30]

Sūtra 7: Multifarious Nature of the Soul

Introduction:

By proper understanding of the true nature of the soul, one

gets liberation (*mukti*). Through the incorrect knowledge of the soul, one is enmeshed in *saṁsāra* (a series of births and deaths). Hence, the true nature of the soul is analysed piecemeal (*tilaśaḥ*)

The Sūtra

7. *sa caiko dvirūpas trimayaś*
caturātmā sapta-pañcaka-svabhāvaḥ[31] /

Translation:

Though he (Ātman) is one, he is two-fold, three-fold, four-fold in form, and is of the nature of seven pañcakas (Pentads).

(1) From the point of our decision, god Śiva who is of the nature of *Cit* (Cidātmā) is the Ātman only. None else, for the light of consciousness is not divisible by Time and Space. *Jaḍa* (material or inert) cannot be the subject of experience but can only be the object.

(2) It is two-fold in form viz. The manifester or the light of consciousness and limited manifestation.[32]

(3) It becomes three-fold as it is mired by the three *malas* pertaining to *aṇu, karma* and *māyā.*

(4) It assumes the nature of (i) śūnya (void i.e. one whose field of experience is void as in the case of *pralaya-kevalī* or *śūnya-pramātā*) (ii) of *prāṇa* (iii) of *puryaṣṭaka* (the subtle body or *sūkṣma śarīra*—a city—consisting of five *tanmātras, manas, buddhi* and *ahaṁkāra*) and (iv) the gross body

(5) Seven pentads i.e. (7×5) 35 *tattvas* from Śiva down to the earth.
From Śiva down to *sakala* (souls)—the consciousness consists of seven experiences viz. (i) (1)Śiva Pramātā, (2) Mantra Maheśvara, (3) Mantreśvara, (4) Mantra, (5) Vijñānakala, (6) Pralayākala, and (7) Sakala
(ii) its essential nature is five-fold viz *cit, ānanda* (bliss), *icchā* (will), *jñāna* (knowledge), *kriyā* (action) but owing to *akhyāti* (ignorance) it becomes limited by the coverings of *kalā, vidyā, rāga, kāla* and *niyati.*

When one realizes that Śiva is the only Reality who becomes thirty-five principles, seven *pramātās* and the pentad of five powers, one is liberated. The ignorance of this causes *saṁsāra.*

Sūtra 8: Role of the Ātman

(All Darśanas i.e their fundamental principles)

Kṣema's breadth of outlook becomes evident when he states that the different schools of philosophy are the different positions adopted by the Ātman. He states:

8. *tadbhūmikāḥ sarva-darśana-sthitayaḥ* I

Translation:

The positions of various schools of philosophy are the various positions adopted by the *soul* or *consciousness.*[33]

It is also interesting to note what principles are regarded by Kṣema as the fundamentals of which school of philosophy. These positions of the different schools are like the roles accepted voluntarily by an actor (soul here). The name of the school and it fundamental principle *as stated by Kṣema* are given below:

Name of the School	*Fundamental Principles*
1. Cārvāka	The self is identical with the body
2. Nyāya and Vaiśeṣika	The soul in worldly life is identical with *buddhi*—the substratum of knowledge, etc. In the *Mokṣa* stage, self being devoid of buddhi, is void-like (śūnya-prāya)
3. (Pūrva) Mīmāṁsā	Confined to *buddhi* or what is known as the cognition of 'I' is covered by *upādhis* (limiting conditions of pleasure and pain) is the self
4. Buddhists	Limited to the functions of *buddhi*. Reality is only a continuum (*santāna*) of cognitions.
5. Some Vedāntins	Prāṇa (vital principle) is Ātman
6. Some Vedāntins 7. And Mādhyamikas	*Abhāva* (non-being) the (fundamental) principle[34] which is the same as śūnya of Mādhyamikas.
8. Pāñcarātras	Lord Vāsudeva is the supreme cause. Jīvas (individual souls) are like sparks emanating from Him. As jīvas are the transformations of the highest cause, they believe *avyakta* as the main principle.

9. Sāṅkhyas and allied schools	Like Vijñānakalas (Ātma is pure knowledge but devoid of any action)
10. Vedāntins	Īśvara as the highest principle as the Upaniṣadic statement declares '*ṣat* was in the beginning' (*sadeva idam agra āsit*).
11. Vaiyākaraṇa (Pāṇini-darśana) described by Mādhava in *Sarva-Darśan-Saṅgraha*	Ātman is *śabda-Brahman* in the form of *Paśyantī*—the highest reality of the Sadāśiva stage.
12. Tāntrikas	The *Ātmantattva* is transcendental to the universe.
13. Śāktas (followers of *Kula āmnāya*)	The Ātman pervades the universe i.e. the universe is a form of ātman.
14. Trika (Kṣema's school of philosophy)	The *Ātman* is both immanent in and transcendental to the universe.

There is only one Ātman who pervades all these bhūmikās.[35] Kṣema quotes here the *Svacchanda Tantra* (10.11.41) which says that Vaiṣṇavas and others whose minds are prejudiced by the *vidyā kañcuka*[36] do not know the highest Lord. Those who desire to obtain Mokṣa but who follow non-liberating systems are whirled round by Māyā. He concludes by quoting the *Netra Tantra* (vii. 30): "Those attached to the body as self (Ātman) do not attain the highest Śivahood."

Another Interpretation: New meanings of certain terms:

Darśana—Knowledge; *Sthiti*—'inward restful pose (*viśrānti*) or cessation.' bhūmikā—'means'. As Dr. Jaidev Singh puts it (*Pratyabhijñā-hṛdaya* pp. 70-71)—"The *sthitis* i.e. the inward cessation of all *darśanas* i.e. *all empirical knowledge e.g. experience of external things (such as colour) or an inner experience (like pleasure) becomes a means of manifestation of the essential nature of tat i.e. Śiva.* So whenever the external form of consciousness comes to rest in the essential nature (of the knower) there ensures *saṁhāra*, resting in a condition of internal peace. The new rising on commencement of a series of *saṁvit-santati* (series of various experiences) follows."

Thus the venerable *Turyā* which holds together emanation, maintenance and reabsorption flashes forth ceaselessly. She is ever full inspite of such sending forth and reabsorption. As *Pratyabhijñā-Ṭīkā* puts it: When reabsorbing the objects, Śakti rises (flashes in Her nature) and so she is full.

Thus this venerable (*śakti*) being resorted to more and more, makes her devotee her own gradually.

How Ātman is covered with mala:

The problem raised is; "If the Ātman is so great as described in the previous Sūtra, how is it called an *aṇu* covered with malas, confined with kalā and other kañcukas of Māyā and becomes a *saṁsārin* (whirling in the cycle of births and deaths)?

Sūtra 9

cid-vat tacchakti-saṅkocāt malāvṛtaḥ saṁsārī /

Translation:

The Śakti of the Ātman gets limited and thereby the Ātman which is all consciousness becomes a *saṁsārin* covered with *malas.*[38]

When the Supreme Lord whose essence is *Cit* (consciousness)—*Cidātmā*—conceals his pervasion of non-duality and adopts duality, His powers such as Will-power and others (*tadīya icchādi-śaktayaḥ*) though unlimited appear to be limited. Then he becomes saṁsārin covered by *mala* (*malāvṛtaḥ saṁsārin*).

Thus his will-power of unrestricted freedom assumes limitations and becomes *āṇava mala,* thereby considering himself imperfect.

His power of knowledge becomes limited gradually in this world full of *bheda.* His omniscience is reduced to knowledge of few things. He gets involved in *Māyīya mala* by acquiring *antaḥkaraṇa* (inner-organ) and external-organs. His action-power (*kriyāśakti*) though omnipotent, gradually gets reduced in this world of differentiation. Becoming extremely limited, it is mired with *kārma mala.* Thus the reduction of the original powers to limited powers is as follows:

Original power of the Ātman	*Reduced power (of the limited soul)*
1. Omnipotence (*sarvakartṛtva*)	1. Kalā (limited power)
2. Omniscience (*sarvajñatva*)	2. Vidyā (limited knowledge)
3. Fullness, perfection *pūrṇatva*	3. Rāga (limitation of desire)
4. Eternity (*nityatva*)	4. Kāla (limitation of time or life)
5. Omnipresence (*vyāpakatva*)	5. Niyati (limitation of space) [1-5 are Kañcukas of Māyā]

Thus such an Ātman of impoverished or limited powers is called *saṁsārin*; with powers bloomed fully he becomes *Śiva.*[39]

Sūtra 10: Śiva-like Five Functions of the Soul

Objection: You say that the Ātman in the stage of *saṁsārin* is Śiva. But is there any proof or appropriate sign or token of his Śivahood in that stage as *saṁsārin*?

Reply: The Sūtra

10. tathāpi tadvat pañca-kṛtyāni karoti ।

Translation:

Even in that condition (of being the limited self or Jīvātman) he performs the five special functions (*pañca-kṛtyāni*) (like Śiva)[40].

Kṣema explains: The Brahman of Vedāntins is inactive. But in *Īśvarādvayavāda*, Śiva whose essence is consciousness, performs the following five activities (as noted in *Svacchanda Tantra* 1.3 while paying obeisance to Śiva). Śiva brings about (i) *sṛṣṭi* (creation of the universe); (ii) *saṁhāra* (re-absorption of the universe); (iii) *vilaya* (concealment); (iv) *sthiti* (maintenance of the world); and (v) *anugraha* (grace).[41] In the *Īśvara Pratyabhijñā* (I.VI.7) it is said that the Lord whose form is consciousness enters into the body etc. and performs the following five actions:

(1) When his attention becomes external, He makes objects (like blue things etc.) appear in definite space-time context. This appearance of objects in definite space and time is his creativeness (sraṣṭṛtā).

(2) With the appearance of the objects in another space-time context, it is His act of absorption *(saṁhartṛtā)*.

(3) With reference to the actual continuity of these objects, it is His maintenance (*sthāpakatā*).

(4) It is His act of concealment (*vilaya-kāritā*) when the objects appear as different.

(5) When everything appears identical with the light of consciousness, it is the act of grace. They explain that in the matter of knowledge, the object of knowledge becomes identical with the knowing subject.

The most important point to be noted here is a way of liberation from *Saṁsāra*. It is that by pondering over the five-fold activity within one's own personal experience steadily, with firm understanding, one realizes the greatness of the Lord.

In other words, one who ponders over these five activities of the Lord and understands that the universe is the unfolded essential nature of the consciousness, become liberated. Those who do not meditate this way remain bound permanently.[42]

Esoteric Pañca Kṛtyas (of a Yogin)

In addition to Pañca Kṛtyas (five acts) mentioned in the previous Sūtra, there is another method.

Sūtra 11

ābhāsana-rakti-vimarśana-bījāvasthāpana-vilāpanatastāni I

To this shall be added : *He performs these. He performs manifestation (ābhāsana), Enjoyment (rakti), Experiencing within oneself (vimarśana), sowing seeds (bījāvasthāpana) and dissolution (vilāpana).*[43]

These five acts are from the point of the spiritual experience of a Yogin. In a nutshell, the esoteric experience of a Yogi corresponds to Śiva's acts as follows:

Śiva's Five Acts	*Yogin's esoteric experience*
1. sṛṣṭi	1. ābhāsana
2. sthiti	2. rakti
3. saṁhāra	3. vimarśana
4. vilaya	4. bījāvasthāpana
5. anugraha	5. vilāpana

The experiences of Yogi are from the highest i.e esoteric point of view.

(1) *sṛṣṭi: (ābhāsana)*: Appearance through the expansion or function of (deities of) perception, hearing etc. (of an object).

(2) *sthiti : rakti :* Enjoying the emanated object with steady or unwinking eyes.

(3) *saṁhāra :* vimarśana

After relishing that object for some time (the *sthiti* position) it is withdrawn at the time of *vimarśa*. Another term for *vimarśa* is *camatkāra*—an intuitive flash of artistic experience. This is called *saṁhāra*.

(4) *vilaya: bījāvasthāpana* : If at the time of *saṁhāra*, the object of experience generates *saṁskāras* or impression (e.g. doubt) then it germinates as *saṁsāra* and imposes the

state of *vilaya* on the Jīvātman resulting in the concealment of the real nature of Jīvātman.

(5) *anugraha* : When the world of germinal form (mentioned above) is burnt to sameness by the process called *haṭhapāka* and by *alaṁgrāsa*, then thus reaching perfection, the Yogī enters the state of *anugraha*.

Here two technical terms are used: *haṭhapāka* and *alaṁ-grāsa*. One more term is *praśama* which means complete reduction of the world of experience to identity with the experient (individual soul).

There are two methods of bringing about *praśama*. Out of these, *śānti praśama* is a slow process while *Haṭhapāka* is a forcible, persistent process.

alaṁ-grāsa : *alaṁ* - full, leaving no germ or impression of *saṁsāra* as separate from consciousness.

grāsa is *ātmasāt-karaṇam* : making it identical with the self.

Kṣema is conscious of the esoteric nature of this process and so advises to approach a competent guru whose guidance is necessary for the experience of such esoteric five-fold act.[44]

Sūtra 12: What is saṁsāritva (state of being involved in saṁsāra)

In concluding the last Sūtra, Kṣema advises to resort to a competent *guru* in order to realize the experience of *pañca-kṛtya-kāritva* described in that Sūtra. If he does not get the guidance from a good *guru*, he does not get a thorough knowledge of his own authorship of these five-fold act. The real nature of his powers (*śaktis*) remains unknown to him. His very powers delude him and make him a *saṁsārin*.

The Sūtra

tad aparijñāne sva-śaktibhir vyāmohitatā saṁsāritvam /

Translation:

This Sūtra explains who is a *saṁsārin*: *Saṁsārin* is one who is deluded by his own powers because he does not know that he is the author or performer of the (Śiva-like) five-fold act.[45]

Kṣema explains: The five acts (mentioned previously) of which he (individual soul) is the author, are always taking place. But due to non-manifestation of one's powers, one is ignorant about them. It is due to the descent of *śakti* that his powers become effective.

It is due to the delusion caused by these (his) *śaktis* that he becomes a *saṁsārin*. These delusions are caused by doubts created by *śāstras*.

It is said: Letters or sounds constitute mantras and the essence of all sounds or letters is Śiva.[46]

Kṣema explains the nature of *parāvāk*, the supreme power of speech. It is not different from the light of *Cit* (consciousness) or Śiva. It is of the form of a *mahāmantra* which is ever risen (i.e. is resonant within eternally). It is the consciousness of the I-ness (*pūrṇāham vimarśamayī*). It is pregnant with the group of *śaktis* presiding over the letters of alphabet beginning with *a* and ending with *kṣa*. It shows the limited self, the successive stages (of speech called) *paśyantī* and *madhyamā*.

When the soul is in a limited condition, *vāk* hides from him her *parā* form. Every moment she creates in that māyā-dominated soul, new *vikalpas* of objects that are obscure (*asphuṭa*) and special (*asādhāraṇa*). Though she is pure, she conceals her real *avikalpa* stage by her *vikalpa* activity.

It is presumed that the following *śaktis* preside over the following classes of alphabet:

Class of alphabet	*Presiding Deity*
1. ka (kha, ga, gha, ṅ)	Brāhmī
2. ca—varga (cha, ja, jha, ñ)	Māheśvarī
3. ṭa—(ṭha, ḍa, ḍha, ṇ)	Kaumārī
4. ta—(tha, da, dha, n)	Vaiṣṇavī
5. pa—(pha, ba, bha, m)	Vārāhī
6. ya—(ra, la, va)	Indrāṇī
7. śa, ṣa, sa	Cāmuṇḍā
8. a (all vowels)	Mahālakṣmī

These *śaktis* deluded the empirical subject to believe that limited objects like body, *prāṇa* etc. are the Self *(Ātman)*. In this *paśu* stage these deities manifest the creation and continuance of *bheda* (difference) and make him fit for only limited *vikalpas*.

But in the *pati* stage, these very *śaktis* withdraw the (sense of) differentiation (*bheda*). They exhibit and retain *abheda* (non-difference or one-ness in all). It gradually decreases the *vikalpas* and enables him (i.e. Jīvātman) to enter into *Bhairavī mudrā*[47] and *śaktis* create *pure vikalpa śakti.* (*a-vikalpa-bhūmi*). This enables the Jīvātman to realize that all this glory of manifestation is his and the whole of the universe is his Ātman. He attains the status of the great Lord though some *vikalpas* may be surviving.[48] [The above is *śāṁbhava upāya*]

Thus the state of a *saṁsārin* (one involved in *saṁsāra*) is nothing but the delusion caused by his own *śaktis*.

The second technique is called *śākta*. Before we proceed it is necessary to classify some terms. '*Śakti*' means 'power', 'energy'. The name given to the *śakti* here is '*Vāmeśvarī*'. She is so named as she 'vomits' ($\sqrt{}$*vam*—to vomit) i.e. brings out the universe out of the Absolute.

Vāmeśvarī has the following sub-species of *śaktis*: *khecarī*, *gocarī*, *dikcarī*, and *bhūcarī*.

(1) *khecarī*—One who moves in the *ākāśa*, a symbol of consciousness. She is connected with the individual soul (*pramātā*) or the empirical subject. The Ātman is an omniscient consciousness. But on account of *khecarī cakra*, the Ātman is reduced to the position of a knower of limited knowledge or experience.

(2) *gocarī*—go implies movement as it means 'rays of light, sense-organs.' *Antaḥkaraṇa* 'the inner-organ', monitors the movements of organs. It is thus a centre of movements, the dynamic apparatus of the individual soul. Hence, *gocarī* is credited with connection with *antaḥkaraṇa*.

(3) *dikcarī*—Literally it means the *śakti* that moves outside in directions or space, Our outer organs (*bahiṣkaraṇa*) are concerned with the consciousness of the outside world. Hence, they constitute the sphere of *dikcarī*.

(4) *bhūcarī*— $\sqrt{}$*bhū*,'to be', 'to exist'. This *śakti* is concerned with existence, 'the world' or external objects (*Bhāvas*). This *śakti* confines the Jīvātman to *bhāvas* or external objects.

These *śakticakras* are concerned with the psycho-physical powers, objects of experience of the individual soul (the experient).

Now let us see the technique of *śākta upāya* as explained by Kṣema:

The divine consciousness-power (*citi-śakti*) is called Vāmeśvarī. It is so designated due to her two different functions. The first, derived from the Sk. $\sqrt{}$*vam*—'to vomit', 'to bring out from one's stomach'. She brings out the universe out (of her belly).

The other meaning is opposite, contrary. She carries out two contrary functions. When the Jīvātman is in the *paśu* stage, it displays itself completely as the pramātā (empirical subject) in its form of *khecarī*, as internal-organ (*antaḥkaraṇa*) in the form of *gocarī*, as outer sense-organs, in the form of *dikcarī* and as external objects or existents in the form of *bhūcarī*.

Then it conceals its real nature as *cid-gagana-carī* (moving in the firmament of consciousness) and through *khecarī*, it limits the power of action (of the Ātman). Through the *gocarī* group, it appears as *antaḥkaraṇa* for ascertaining difference (*bheda-niścaya*), as *buddhi* for deciding things as different (*bheda-vikalpana*) and as *manas* (mind) to ascertain non-difference. It appears through *dikcarī* group, the deity of outer senses whose function is to perceive differences. It appears through *bhūcarī* group in the form of differential knowable objects.

Thus *Vāmeśvarī* hides the real nature of the self and deludes the hearts of beings. *Vāmeśvarī* who does this to a *pramātā* in the *paśu* stage, does the contrary of it, when he reaches the *pati* stage.

When the Pramātā reaches the *pati* stage, the Vāmeśvarī transforms herself in *cid-gaganeśvarī* whose main characteristic is omnipotence; as *gocarī* she ascertains non difference; as *dikcarī* she perceives non-difference and as *Bhūcarī* she reveals external objects as parts of one's body.

Here Kṣema quotes Bhaṭṭa Dāmodara who concludes that the state of *saṁsārin* is that of being deluded by ones own *śaktis*.[49]

Āṇavopāya

The supreme Lord has a unique *aiśvarya śakti*. It is the sovereign power of the Lord. Its essential nature is the ability to do anything—*kartṛtā* or *vimarśa* which is essentially *sphurattā* (flashing forth) or *prakāśa*. This *aiśvarya-śakti* conceals her real nature and deludes the *pramātā* in the *paśu* stage i.e. when he is a *saṁsārin* (one who is a victim of the cycle of births and deaths).

She does so by her powers (*śaktis*) called *prāṇa*, *apāna* and *samāna*.

At this point, these Trika terms must be distinguished from what is given usually in yoga works. According to Patañjali, *prāṇa, apāna, samāna, udāna* and *vyāna* are vital airs and not *śaktis* as in Trika Śaivism. Yogī Yājñavalkya[50] gives the following

functions of vital airs called *prāṇa* etc.
Prāṇa—Functions: To breathe, to digest food. Its position—From heart to nose, controls upper organs.
Apāna—Function: Easing out of urine, discharge of faeces—Position: From navel to feet, controls lower organs. Natural tendency to go downwards.
Samāna—Position: From navel to heart. Function: Distribution of the digested food to all sense-organs and *nāḍīs*.
Vyāna—Function: Blood-circulation and activating *nāḍīs*. Place: All over the body.
Udāna—Place: Throat. It transfers the subtle body of a person to the next birth or incarnation.[51]

As stated above, Kṣema regards *prāṇas* as *śaktis* and not vital airs. Their functions are somewhat different[52] from those given in Patañjali. It is a comprehensive term covering all the functions of life. *Prāṇa* is the vital *vāyu* that goes out (?) while *apāna* is the vital *vayu* that goes downwards towards the anus. *Samāna* is located in the interior of the body and helps assimilation of food equitably.
Vyāna means going in all directions; it is everywhere in the body. *Udāna* means, going up. By means of *prāṇa*, *apāna* and *samāna śaktis*, the individual soul gets bound—a *paśu* and by *udāna* and *vyāna śaktis*, one becomes freed—a *pati*.

Except the functions of *vāyus* or *śaktis* to bind and free the individual soul, there is not much difference in the concepts of these schools except the use of the term '*śakti*' instead of '*vāyu*'.

Now when the *aiśvarya-śakti* binds the individual soul by *prāṇa*, *apāna* and *samāna śakti*, by states such as waking, dream and sleep by organs of the body, *prāṇa* and *puryaṣṭaka* (subtle body consisting of five *Tanmātras, Manas, Buddhi* and *Ahaṁkāra*) and thus makes him (the individual soul) *saṁsārin*. When she unfolds the *udāna śakti* in the *suṣumṇā nāḍī* (called here *madhya-dhāma*, of middle position between *Iḍā* and *Piṅgalā Nāḍī* which flow in the left and the right nostrils and is of the nature of *Turyā* (the fourth state after sleep) and when she unfolds her world pervading *vyāna śakti* and is of the nature of Turyātīta (beyond, higher than Turyā state) one reaches the stage of *pati* or Śivahood and is a liberated soul while alive.

Thus the words '*sva-śaktibhir vyāmohitatā*' (being deluded by one's own *śaktis*) are explained in three ways.

Kṣema refers here to Sūtra No.9 which states : "When the light of consciousness assumes limitation, one becomes a *saṁsārin*". The same is stated here: "One who gets deluded by one's own *śaktis* becomes a *saṁsārin*". The Āgama also declares: "They (all individual souls) are the supreme Lords incognito, when they enter the body.[53]"

Abhinava (?) stated in the *Pratyabhijñā Ṭīkā:*
They who realize their body, a jar or thirtysix Tattvas are a form of Śiva become siddhas (or reach perfection).[54]

Sūtra 13: Citta becomes Citi.

Kṣema wishes to emphasize the real insight into the essence of the Truth by a converse sūtra.

The Sūtra

13: tat parijñāne cittam eva antar-mukhī-bhāvena cetana-padādhyārohāt citiḥ ।

Translation:

When the full knowledge (of the doership or activity of the five-fold act of the individual soul) is realized, *citta* (individual consciousness) itself becomes *Citi* (universal consciousness) by turning within, due to its rise to the status of *Cetana.*[55]

Kṣema explains every word of the sūtra as follows:

Tat—tasya: the authorship of the five activities (pañca kṛtyas) by the self.
Parijñāna—Thorough knowledge (literally, the delusion caused by one's own *śaktis* is removed).
Citta attains *svātantrya* and abandons its limiting tendency and becomes inward looking (*antarmukhī-bhāvena*) and gradually attains the status of *Cetana* (the perfect or uncontracted consciousness) of a knowing subject. Thereby the limitation aspect disappears and its real nature is attained. It enters its highest stage.

Thus Citta becomes Citi.

Introduction:
The previous sūtra states that *Citi-śakti* in its highest aspect 'devours' (eliminates) all differences. It should do so even in

the stage when it is covered by Māyā, just as the sun though covered by clouds continues to manifest objects.

Sūtrakāra replies:[56]

14 citi-vahniḥ avarohapade channo'pi I
mātrayā meyendhanam pluṣyati I

Translation:

The fire (the capacity to burn—eliminate all differences) of *Citi*, even in its lower stage (i.e. even when covered or conditioned by Māyā) continues to consume (burn) partly (the fuel in the form of the known objects).

Kṣema explains: *Citi* is compared here to fire. Just as fire burns (assimilates to itself), though slowly and partly, the fuel, even if it is covered with ashes, the *māyā pramātā* (individual soul conditioned by Māyā) burns i.e. assimilates to itself the fuel in the form of objects of knowledge partly (*mātrayā*).

The trika theory is: objects when known, become assimilated with the consciousness and their difference gets annihilated. But this assimilation is partial, not complete. It makes them rise again by the *saṁskāras* (i.e. impression of the objects left on the mind).

Utpaladeva says in *Śiva-stotrāvali*: "Since all creatures (even gods) go on devouring (i.e. assimilating), O God, I pay obeisance to the universe which is your own form".[57]

"All conscious beings go on devouring (experiencing and assimilating objects) I bow down to the universe as you constantly assimilate it to yourself."

Sūtra 15 : Introduction:

Now Kṣema (Sūtrakāra) explains what happens when the *pramātā* develops within himself the *prasāra* (expansion) of the (divine) sense and adopts the technique (*yukti*) of the practice of creation (*sarga*) or emanation (of the objective existence) and also that of *saṅkoca* (withdrawing of the senses)—and thus adopt the technique of *saṁhāra* (withdrawal of objectivity of the world).

The Sūtra

15. bala-lābhe viśvam ātmasāt karoti I

Translation:

The Sūtrakāra replies: The Pramātā acquires the inherent power of bala of the *Citi* and assimilates to himself the whole of the universe.

Kṣema explains: What is *bala* (power)?: '*Citi*' submerges the covering of the body, *Prāṇa* etc. It then exhibits prominently its essential nature. It thus emerges as *bala.*

When this power of consciousness is acquired and one exhibits his newly attained real nature, one makes the universe identical with one's self (literally—one makes the universe from Sadāśiva to the earth, one's own). Here Kṣema quotes *Krama-sūtra* which states: "Just as fire ablaze consumes the fuel, so one should burn objects which are like fetters.[59]

He further quotes *Pratyabhijñā:* It is not correct to say that this all-inclusiveness of *citi* of assimilating the whole of the universe (*samāveśa*) is temporary (*kādācitkī*). The temporariness is due to appearance and disappearance (*un-majjana* and *ni-majjana*) of the body, *Prāṇa* etc. It is the supreme Will of *Citi* which manifests the body etc. which makes to appear the all-inclusive nature of *Citi* as temporary. This all-inclusive role is eternally manifest. If *Citi* were not ever in manifestation, even the body would not appear as objects of universal consciousness.[60] The Yogic practice is advised so that the false identification of the individual soul with the body should be removed. It is not for attaining the experience of consciousness which by its nature is forever shining.[61]

Sūtra 16: What is Jīvan-mukti?

The Sūtra:

> 16. *cidānanda-lābhe dehādiṣu cetyamāneṣvapi cidaikātmya-pratipatti-dārḍhyam jīvan-muktiḥ* ।

Translation:

The state when the bliss of *Cit* (cidānanda) is attained and the consciousness of identity with *Cit* is stabilized, even when one is alive (literally—while the body etc. are being experienced) is called *Jīvan-mukti.*[62]

Kṣema explains: One attains the bliss of *Cit* (*cidānanda*) when one enters into *samāveśa* or *samādhi.* In that state, the entire universe appears as one's own self (literally—the whole universe is experienced as identical with the self) and the consciousness of empirical self disappears. Though the *samādhi* state is over, that is, in the *vyutthāna* state, one experiences that external objects (such as blue, body or *Prāṇa*) and internal states (such as pleasure, pain etc.) are mere coverings. The impressions of the unity consciousness (with *Cit*) left during the *samādhi* period is so indelible that the experience of unity conscious with *Citi* are permanent. This firmness of consciousness of identity with *Cit* is *Jīvan-mukti* or liberation while one is alive. For as a result of the recognition of one's real nature, all the shackles of ignorance melt away (are destroyed). Kṣema quotes Vasugupta in support of this view : "He who realizes thus that the universe is identical with the self and regards the whole world as a (divine) sport is liberated during his life as he is permanently united with the universal consciousness."[63]

Sūtra 17: Cidānanda-lābha

Introduction:

After discussing the importance of *Cidānanda*—the bliss of *Cit*—Kṣema proceeds to explain how to secure it.

The Sūtra

17 madhya-vikāsāt cidānanda-lābhaḥ ।

Translation:

Cidānanda is secured by the expansion or development of the madhya.[64]

A bit of digression to explain the term Madhya:

(1) *Madhya*—The glorious consciousness (*bhagavatī saṁvid*). From Śiva's point of view, it is the universal consciousness, the innermost central reality of all existence. Without being attached to it as the support, nothing can exist. The dictum is that at first *saṁvit* is transformed into *Prāṇa.*[65]

(2) In the stage of Māyā, the *saṁvid* conceals her real nature. It assumes the role of *Prāṇa-śakti* into *Mahāprāṇa,* the primal energy as distinguished from ordinary *prāṇa* (vital air).

(3) From the point of the individual soul, it is called *Madhya-nāḍī* or *Madhyamā-Nāḍī*. Kṣema tells us that its substratum is Brahman in the form of *prāṇa-śakti* right from the *Brahmarandhra* (cerebral aperture) down to *adho-vaktra* (anus). It is like the central rib of a *palāśa* leaf. It is called *Madhya-nāḍī*, because all functions begin from it and come to rest in it.

(4) Though the individuals are not aware of it, *Madhya Nāḍī* is *Suṣumṇā* and is designated so, as it is between the two *nāḍīs*—*iḍā* (to the right) and *Piṅgalā* to the left. It passes through the *merudaṇḍa* (the cerebro-spinal axis). It extends from *Mūlādhāracakra* (spinal centre of the region below genitals) and extends to *Sahasrāra Cakra* (cerebral plexus).

The Trika Śivas add: The *Suṣumṇā* or *Madhya Nāḍī* is of three types—*Tāmasika*, *Rājasika* and *Sāttvika* (according to the *Triguṇa* theory of Sāṅkhyas).

The *Tāmasika Suṣumṇā* is fiery red. Within this *Nāḍī* is the lustrous *Rājasika Vajrā* or *Vajriṇī Nāḍī* brilliant like the sun. Within the *Rājasika Vajriṇi* is *Sāttvika* or *Citrā /Citriṇī Nāḍī* of moonlike lustre. In the interior of the *Citriṇī* is the *Brahma Nāḍī*. The opening of the *Citriṇī* is the *Brahmadvāra*. It is through this *Nāḍī* that *Kuṇḍalinī* climbs upto *Brahmarandhra*.

It is regarded that these three parallel *Nāḍīs* start from the *Mūlādhāra Cakra* and join together at *Ājñācakra* in the middle of eyebrows.

Now let us turn to the Sūtra 17

As most of the commentary of the sūtra is incorporated in the above description of *Nāḍīs*, the commentary of the *Sūtra*, may be summarised as follows:

The *Bhagavatī Saṁvit* is the innermost reality of all forms or things. Without the support of this *saṁvit* nothing can exist. Though *saṁvit* is the innermost reality and the support of everything, it hides its real nature in the *Māyā* stage. It accepted the role of *mahāprāṇa* as distinguished from ordinary vital airs (*prāṇa*). It rests on *Buddhi*, *Prāṇa* and followed the path of the thousand nāḍīs. Even as individual embodiment, it remains chiefly as *Madhyama-Nāḍī* (Suṣumṇā). Its substructure is Brahman in the form *Prāṇa-śakti* extending from the cerebral aperture to the anus. It is called *Madhyamā* (central) *Nāḍī* as all functions take their origin from it and return for rest therein.

When the *saṁvit* (consciousness) is developed by the practice of *Pañcakṛtyas* or the development of the *Brahma-nāḍī* takes place (by methods prescribed later), the bliss of *Cit* (the universal consciousness) is achieved and *Jīvan-mukti* (liberation even while alive) is attained.

Sūtra 18: The Techniques of Madhya-vikāsa

[*Guidance of a competent guru is essential for these*]
In Sūtra 18, Kṣem. mentions various techniques of mastering *madhya-vikāsa.*

The sūtra is as follows:

18 *vikalpa-kṣaya-śakti-saṅkoca-vikāsa-vāhaccheda-ādyantakoṭi-nibhālanādaya ihopāyaḥ* I

Translation:

Here the means are as follows: elimination of *vikalpas, saṅkoca* and *vikāsa* of *śaktis,* practice of concentrating on the two extremes of breath at the beginning and at the end and others.

The following are the techniques of developing the centre (*Madhya*):

(1) *Vikalpa-kṣaya*—elimination of vikalpas
(2) *Saṅkoca* and *Vikāsa of śaktis*
(3) *Vāha-ccheda*—cutting of *vāha* (breath)
(4) *Ādyanta-koṭi-nibhālana*—practice of concentration on the two extremes of breath. And such others are the *upāyas* (means) of the development of the *madhya.*

Previously, it has been explained that performing the pañca-kṛtyas—five Śiva-like activities, at individual level have been advised for unfoldment of the central *Śakti.* Here the following methods are prescribed:

1. *Vikalpa-kṣaya:* This is given priority not merely because it is prescribed in *Īśvara-Pratyabhijñā* (IV.1.11.B), but also because the restrictions of rigorous disciplines (of *Haṭha Yoga*) such as *Prāṇāyāma, Mudrā, Bandha,* etc. are 'shattered.'[66]

One should concentrate his *citta* (individual consciousness) on the *saṁvid* or *Cit.* He should not think of anything else and restrain *vikalpas.* By such practice one reaches non-vikalpa state. He thus gets used to regard *Cit* as unconnected with the body. Shortly he gets absorbed in *Turyā* and the *Turyātīta* state—a state in which the whole universe appears as one's own self. In this state *vyāna śakti* is active. Utpaladeva says: "One gradually attains the divine state of *Īśvara* by banning *vikalpas* and concentration of mind."[67] Vasugupta in *Spanda Kārikā* (I.9) also states that the highest state is attained when the mental agitation (due to *vikalpas*) calms down (dissolves).[68]

2. *Saṅkoca-vikāsa of śakti:* Though this technique is not taught in the *Pratyabhijñā* doctrine, it has the sanction of *Āmnāya* (sacred tradition). Kṣema describes some more techniques in the hope that a person should enter into *samādhi* by using one of them.

Before we proceed, it is necessary to understand the implications of the technical terms used by Kṣema.

(i) Saṅkoca of śaktis: Just as a tortoise contracts all its limbs within itself in case of fear, one should withdraw the consciousness which goes out to external objects through the sense-organs, and should turn it towards the Ātman (self). This reverting of sense-organs to the self is *un-mukhī-karaṇa.* The self is ever present as a resting place.

(ii) Vikāsa: The hidden śaktis are simultaneously going through the openings of all sense-organs.[69]

This technique of inner absorption with external expansion of the sense is called *Bhairavī Mudrā* in which while the external sight is steady without blinking, object of one's aspiration is to be seen within.[70]

Kallaṭa, a disciple of Vasugupta says, "*Vikāsa* of *Madhya śakti* is accomplished by transformation *(pariṇāmataḥ)*".[71]

There are two more terms connected with *saṅkoca* and *vikāsa.*

(iii) Kuṇḍalinī: Kuṇḍalinī is a śakti which is supposed to lie folded up in three and a half coils in the *Mūlādhāra Cakra.* When she rises with half of her length (one-three fourth of her coils), she goes up through *suṣumṇā,* crosses *Laṁbikā* and proceeds to *Brahmarandhra.* Kuṇḍalinī, pervading the upper part of *Laṁbikā* is called *ūrdhva kuṇḍalinī.* This pervasion is called *vikāsa* or *viṣa* ($\sqrt{}$*viṣ*—to pervade).

(iv) Laṁbikā: Laṁbikā is the cross-road of four *Nāḍīs* or channels of *Prāṇa*. Its position is near the palate. The first two channels (*iḍā* and *piṅgalā*) are the conduit for all ordinary *Jīvas*. Through the third channel the Yogin starts from *Mūlādhāra Cakra* and rises through *ūrdhva kuṇḍalinī* upto *Brahmarandhra*. The fourth is meant for advanced Yogins who do not require to pass through Mūlādhāra and rise straight to the *Brahmarandhra*.
(v) Adhaḥ-kuṇḍalinī: From *Laṁbikā* downwards to *Mūlādhāra Cakra*, the one-three-fourth coils or length of the Kuṇḍalinī spreads and through that (*adhaḥ kuṇḍalinī*) Prāṇa goes to the *Mūlādhāra Cakra. Meḍhra kanda* is below the *Mūlādhāra*, near the root of the rectum. When Prāṇa enters *adhaḥ kuṇḍalinī*, it is the *saṅkoca*. It is also called *Vahni* ($\sqrt{}$*vah*—to carry) as Prāṇa through suṣumṇā is carried down to *Mūlādhāra*.
(vi) Ṣaṣṭha vaktra: The five *vaktras* i.e. mouths or openings are—two ears, two eyes, mouth and anus. *Meḍhra kanda*, below *Mūlādhāra* is the sixth organ (not a 'mouth').

After understanding the above concepts, Kṣema's description of this technique may be summarised as follows (the wording of the *Sūtra* is given above and its explanation follows):

Śakteḥ saṅkocaḥ—The *śakti* (consciousness) that spreads out through the 'gates' of sense-organs to external objects is to be withdrawn and reverted to the Ātman (*un-mukhī karaṇam*). Here he quotes a mantra from *Kaṭhopaniṣad* which really belongs to the Black Yajurveda but Kṣema associates it with the *Atharva*.[72] It means: "The Self-born Lord created openings (sense-organs) to the body through which one looks to outward world not to the soul. But a wise man reverts his sight inwards, sees the soul (*Pratyagātman*) and attains (lit. *tastes*) immortality."

About '*saṅkoca*' he gives the illustration of an endangered tortoise withdrawing its limbs simultaneously and advises the aspirant to do so (with regard to his *śaktis*) and rest in the ever-shining Ātman.

Śakteḥ vikāsaḥ: As *Kakṣyā-stotra* addressed to Śiva[73] explains: The powers of seeing etc. are to be forced out, by will-power, simultaneously, on all sides into their respective objects and remaining undisturbed within like a (golden) pillar (Oh, Lord you appear as the support of the universe).

This technique of inner absorption with external expansion is stated above as *Bhairavī Mudrā*. The *vikāsa* means the practice of expansion and resting of *śakti* in the *ūrdhva-kuṇḍalinī* by gradual restraint of Prāṇa between the eyebrows. The restraint is mastered by the power of subtle Prāṇa. This subtle Prāṇa gradually develops by regulating the vibration in the pair of nostrils.

The location of *adhaḥ-kuṇḍalinī* is the *Meḍhra kanda*. After entering into *Suṣumṇā*, Prāṇa is carried down into the *Adhaḥ Kuṇḍalinī* its root, end and the middle. The entrance of Prāṇa into *adhaḥ-kuṇḍalinī* is the *saṅkoca* of *Prāṇa śakti* or the *vahni*. Kṣema quotes the *Vijñānabhairava* which advises to concentrate (Lit. throw) the delighted *citta* in the middle of the *Vahni* (i.e. the *saṅkoca* stage) and *viṣa* (i.e. *vikāsa* stage) whether by itself or filled by *Prāṇic vāyu* and enjoy the bliss of sexual intercourse.[74]

Here the term *viṣa* indicates the *vikāsa* stage and *vahni* the *saṅkoca* stage when Prāṇa rises into *ūrdhva kuṇḍalinī*, it is *vikāsa*.

The *āveśa* or entrance of *Prāṇa* in the *adhaḥ-kuṇḍalinī* is *saṅkoca*.

To sum up :

When the *Prāṇa* and *Apāna* enter the *Suṣumṇā*, the *citta* (individual consciousness) should be retained in between *ūrdhva-kuṇḍalinī* and *adhaḥ-kuṇḍalinī*.

Vāhaccheda

This technique is related to breath control or *prāṇāyāma*. The word '*vāha*' means 'carrier', 'breath'. When we inhale fully, our breath reaches upto the final point (somewhere near the heart) where it automatically stops slightly and exhalation of breath begins. It reaches (outside) to a distance of twelve *aṅgulas*. At this last point, the breath stops a bit and inhalation of breath begins. The highest point of inhalation is called *hṛt* and last point of exhalation is called '*dvādaśāṅgula*', '*dvādaśānta*' or simply '*dvādaśa*' to denote its length or extension.

The term *vāhaccheda* means 'cutting' that is 'the stopping' of the two *vāhas*, *Prāṇa* and *Apāna*, which flow through the right and left nostrils. This process is natural. But Kṣema attributes it to the pronunciation of sound of consonants like *k*, *h* without any vowel (the term *an-ac-ka* means without (*an*) any vowel (*ac*, as Pāṇini used for all vowels like *a*, *i*, etc.). This is obviously an unuttered state of mantras. Thus both *Prāṇa* and *Apāna* rest at the heart. He substantiates by quoting a verse from *Jñāna-garbha*[75].

Kṣema calls '*hṛt*' or '*hṛdaya*' as the first point (*ādi-koṭi*) and *dvādaśānta* as the last point (*anta-koṭi*). And *nibhālana* is the practice of concentrating the mind on these two points.

Kṣema aptly quotes *Vijñānabhairava* (4a) which states that the fickleness or fluctuation of the mind goes on decreasing every moment only if one concentrates (lit. 'throws') one's mind wheresoever and howsoever on *dvādaśānta*.[76] This is also stated in *Spanda Kārikā*, but here Kṣema quotes a part of *Spanda Kārikā* to explain the term *unmeṣa*. The full verse is given in notes.[77] It means: 'While absorbed in one thought another arises. In between there is rest (absence of thought). To rest mentally on this junction point is *unmeṣa*. One gets the experience of *spanda*, the creative nature of Śiva, at these points.

This is the explanation of *unmeṣa* from *śākta* point of view. But from *śāmbhava* point of view, the emergence of the highest Reality (*Pāramārthikabhāva*) while absorbed in meditation of the Lord is *unmeṣa*.

Kṣema adds one more *śākta* technique in which the aspirant rises to the highest bliss by concentrating on aesthetic enjoyment. That *Dhāraṇā* is prescribed in *Vijñānabhairava* (72-74). They are:

(1) *āsvāda dhāraṇā*—concentration on the flavour of sweets and drinks.
(2) *śabda dhāraṇā*—concentration on melodious music—vocal and instrumental.
(3) *manastuṣṭi dhāraṇā*—concentrating on whatever pleases and satisfies the mind.

To summarise the text of Vijñānabhairava[78]:

(1) At the experience of ecstatic pleasure of tasting the flavour of sweet dishes and drinks, one should meditate on the highest pitch of this pleasure and thus one becomes filled with great bliss.
(2) When a Yogin gets mentally absorbed in melodious music, then, because the Yogin has become one with it, there is identity of the Yogin with that music (*tadātmatā*).
(3) Wherever individual mind takes pleasure it should be allowed to concentrate on that. In every such case

(*tatra tatra*) the real nature of the highest bliss (*parānanda*) flashes forth.

Thus, any other type of blissful meditation on the self should be allowed (*anumantavyam*). These and such other techniques are for development of the *Madhya-Nāḍī* (*suṣumṇā*).

Sutra 19: Permanence of Samādhi

After describing the technique of the development of *Madhya*, one gets the bliss of *cit* (consciousness). It is definitely the *Samādhi* of Supreme Yogins. The words *'samāveśa'*, *samāpatti* are synonyms of *'Samādhi'*.

This sūtra (No.19) explains what should be done for its permanence or 'ever-risen condition' of *samādhi*.

The Sūtra

19 samādhi-saṁskāravati vyutthāne
bhūyo bhūyaścidaikyā marśān
nityodita-samādhi-lābhaḥ[79] ।

Vyutthāna is the normal stage of consciousness after *Samādhi*. *The Sūtra states:*

Translation:

This *(vyutthāna)* stage is built of impressions during the *samādhi*. *Permanent samādhi* can be achieved by constantly brooding over one's identity with *Cit* (universal consciousness).

Kṣema explains: When a great Yogī comes to normal consciousness after *Samādhi*, he is full of the impressions of the *Samādhi* state and 'shakes' to and fro with ecstasy like an intoxicated person. He sees that the mass of objects before him are getting dissolved in the *Cit*-sky (the sky of universal consciousness) like a speck of cloud in the autumnal sky. He resorts now and then to his previous internal *Samādhi*. He considers himself as identical with *Cit* by the process of *Nimīlana Samādhi*[80] in which personal consciousness is merged in the universal consciousness and one becomes identical with it. Even at the time of *Vyutthāna*, he enjoys the bliss of *Samādhi*.

To elaborate this sūtra, Kṣema quotes the following *Krama sūtra*. Here *Krama* does not refer to the Tāntric branch of

Kashmir Śaivism. It means 'series', 'serial', 'sequence'. The Sanskrit Text is as follows:[81]

> *krama-mudrayā antaḥ-svarūpayā bahir-mukhaḥ samāviṣṭo bhavati sādhakaḥ* ।

The meanings of the words:

Mudrā

(1) That which being of the nature of highest bliss, spreads or distributes joy
(2) That which dissolves (*drāvaṇāt*) all bonds
(3) That which seals up the universe into the inner *turīya* stage

Krama—sequence or cycle

(1) It is so-called because it causes creation, maintenance, absorption consecutively as if in a circle.
(2) It consists of their creation etc. in a series—Kṣema

The *Sādhaka*, Yogī or aspirant becomes *samāviṣṭa* (one who has realized the unfolding of the supreme power) even while he is *bahirmukha* (engaged in external objects). In this *Mudrā*, the mind alternates (goes outward and inward) between the internal and external. The internal appears as the universal consciousness and external the form of *Śiva* only—not the world—the supreme power (*parāśakti*) manifests completely in a flash.

> *tatrādau bāhyāt antaḥ praveśaḥ*
> *ābhyantarāt bāhya-svarūpe praveśaḥ*
> *āveśa-vaśāt jāyate iti sabāhyābhyantaro*
> *ayaṁ mudrā kramaḥ*[82] ।

Meaning of words:

bāhya —external sense-objects
bāhyāt— on account of the assimilation of external objects of senses
antaḥ— into highest *Citi* plane i.e. that of universal consciousness

Herein at first, the totality of the external objects is 'devoured' i.e. assimilated into the internal i.e. into the highest *Citi* plane of the universal consciousness. By this process of assimilation, *samāveśa* or entrance into the inwards takes place. "Again through the realization of the nature of *citi* by the power of *samāveśa,* entrance into the external i.e. into the totality of sense-objects appears as this (*idantā*). This entrance (*praveśa*) is also a *samāveśa* of the nature of manifestation of the solidification of the essence of *Cit.*" [as adapted from Jaydev Singh p.105]

This ever-risen (eternally active) *samāveśa* is simultaneously external and internal. It is of the nature of *Mudrā* (as explained above).

Sūtra 20: Blessings of attainment of samādhi

This concluding Sūtra describes the blessing derived from permanent *Samādhi,* attained by *Krama Mudrā.*
The Sūtra counts the blessings as follows:[83]

The Sūtra

20 *tadā prakāśānanda-sāra-mahāmantra-vīryātmaka-pūrṇāhantā āveśāt sadā sarva-sarga-saṁhārakāri-nija-saṁvid-devatā-cakreśvaratā-prāptiḥ bhavati-iti śivam* I

Translation:

When the *Krama Mudrā* is attained (*tadā*) and when one enters into perfect I-consciousness *(pūrṇāhantā)*—a state, an essence of *Cit* (or prakāśa) and *Bliss* (ānanda)—and is the potentiality of great mantras, one attains sovereignty over one's circle of deities of consciousness (*nija-saṁvid-devatā-cakra*) which causes all creation and absorption of the universe.

All this (is the nature of) Śiva.[83]

While elucidating this sūtra, Kṣema explains the terms used in it. The Sūtrakāra says: When one attains permanent or lasting (*nityodita*) *Samādhi,* the supreme Yogin mentioned in this *Prakaraṇa* (text) attains overlordship (*īśvaratā*) over the circle of deities of his consciousness (*nija-saṁvid-devatā-cakra*).[84] This circle of deities always causes the creation and absorption of the universe beginning from Kāla-rudrāgni[85] and culminating in the last (*śāntā*) *Kalā,* by the *Āveśa* (merging or identification of the individual self with the universal (self) into the spontaneous *camatkāra.* It is the essence of *Prakāśa* and *Ānanda* (Bliss),—a dense solid compact of consciousness and bliss (*cid-āhlāda-ekaghana*). It is the vital essence of all mantras (*sarva-mantra-*

jīvita-bhūta). It is perfect (*pūrṇa*) that is of the nature of the highest *Bhaṭṭārikā* (i.e. the highest vimarśa). This is the I-consciousness (*ahantā*).

All this is really Lord Śiva Himself (*iti Śivam*).

Now Kṣema gives the hierarchy in the stages of reality:

(1) *Prameya* or *saṁvedya*— whatever is cognised or known.
(2) *Pramāṇa* or *saṁvedana*—cognition, knowledge.
(3) *Pramātā*—individual souls or experients who are full of consciousness.
(4) *Sadāśiva*—whose sense of identification with the individual body (literally—limiting adjuncts of the body) is 'dissolved' and whose body is the whole universe.
(5) *Maheśvara*—the highest stage of reality. He is full of *camatkāra*—the bliss of perfect consciousness of the entire universe and is identical with his *prakāśa*.

In Kṣema's words: Hence the essence of whatever is perceived (*prameya*) is *pramāṇa* (cognition). Of these *Pramātās* (inward looking individuals) who are full of self-consciousness are the essential truth *(tattvam)*. But of them, those whose perception of identity with the body and other adjuncts *(upādhis)* is lost and whose body is the whole universe, have the status of *Sadāśiva* and *Īśvara*. Lord Maheśvara is the highest reality *(Paramārtha)*. He is full of *camatkāra* or *vimarśa* (the bliss of perfect consciousness of the entire universe). It is rendered so by his identity with *Prakāśa* which is at the basis of all manifestation.

No manifestation is possible unless and until it enters the *Prakāśa* of the supreme Reality, as *Prakāśa* is the source and basis of all manifestations.

And the Supreme Lord, on account of his being the essence of complete freedom, is full of the exuberance of bliss as he is bereft of all desires and is perfect in all respects. He mentally grasps the complete *gamut* of non-Māyīya words.[86] from *a* to *kṣa* and the whole world consisting of *vācaka* (signifier) and *vācya* (the object signified). He has thus achieved (reached) the state of full *Jagadānanda*[87]—the bliss of the self appearing as the universe.

The universe is hence extended, beginning with *a* which is of the nature of all-surpassing (i.e. supreme) *A-kula* (Śiva).[88] He is so designated as He is not the manifestation of *kula* (śakti). From the point of *Mātṛkā-cakra* letters of the alphabet, *a* is Śiva and *ha* is the expansion of *Śakti*, the whole universe is extended. *Kṣa* shows the end of that expansion. By the combination of *a* and *ha* as if in a pair of vowels (that is *a-ha*) in the *Pratyāhāra* fashion that is the mention of the first letter of the sūtra or word only of the last letter,[89] it rests in the form of a *Bindu* which shows the consciousness of non-differentiation.

Thus this is the natural *vimarśa* or inward experience of the nature of *Śabda-rāśi* (mass of words).

Here Kṣema quotes *Ajaḍa-pramātṛ-siddhi* (vv 22-23) in which he defines what is meant by 'feeling of I-ness' (*aham-bhāvaḥ*). It is the rest of all objective experience within oneself. It is called absolute free will (*svātantryam*), ability to do anything (*kartṛtva*) and lordship on everything as all relational consciousness is prohibited.[90] and has not to depend on outside world.

It is hence that *Ahantā* (I-consciousness or 'I-ness') is called the base of great power as it is the source of and place of rest of all mantras and it is by its power that all activities (about objects) are carried out.

He quotes two *Spanda-kārikās* (II. 1-2) in support:[91]

(1) After resorting to the power of spanda—

tattva (viz. *cid-rūpa*) .....Spanda K. II.1

and ending with: All these mantras are of the nature of Śiva.

....Spanda K.II. 2 Even in *Śiva Sūtra* (1.22) it is stated:

One attains the experience of mantra-power by merging in (the great lake *Mahāhrada*). The 'lake' mentioned by Vasugupta in the above sūtra is the deep or infinite supreme spiritual awareness.

Citi-śakti, background of experience

It may be the experience of inner subjects like pleasure (pain, etc.) or of outward objects like blue etc. determined by *Buddhi*, remembered or planned by the mind, it is *Citi-śakti* which flashes forth as the background of all experiences. As it has been remarked: In the absence of the flashing of *Citi* nothing can flash.[92]

While she is thus shining brilliantly, she, by her *Māyā power*, appears variously by assuming the nature of inward and outward objects (like pleasure, pain, blue objects). And the *Māyā-subjects* (individual souls) consider it as knowledge, ideas, resolution

(*Jñāna-saṅkalpa-adhyavasāyādi-rūpatayā*). In fact, this is one and same *Citi-śakti.*

As Utpaladeva, in *Īśvarapratyabhijñā, Jñānādhikāra* (V.18)[93] says:

It is due to the *Māyā śakti* of the all-powerful Lord that Māyā has to function with different knowables and is called knowledge, ideas, determination and other epithets.

To sum up:

It is one and the same *Citi-śakti* which appears in various ways in all conditions

Īśvara-Pratyabhijñā. Jñanādhikāra, *7.1 says:*[94]

"And this consciousness of object (*Pratibhā*) i.e. the consciousness, which shines affected by a succession of a variety of objects is nothing but the great Lord, the subject who is essentially the eternal unchanging light of consciousness." IPV III, p.99

K.C. Pandey's translation

Now *Kṣema explains*: The highest Yogin attains the status of Lordship (*īśvaratā*) and that of the supreme *Bhairava* (*para-bhairavātmatā*). For this the pre-conditions are as follows: To attain *citi-śakti* by entering into and securing firm hold on it (as mentioned in Sūtra 18). After entering into the *Citi-śakti, unmīlana* (blooming, expansion) and *nimīlana* (in-folding, *saṅkoca*) is to be affected in succession. Everything is of the nature of everything in emanation and absorption. Whatever group i.e. *cakra* of natural-consciousness deities (*sahajā - saṁvitti - devatā*)— the *non-māyīya* group of internal and external sense-organs, which goes on forever with projection and withdrawal, the Yogi acquires overlordship over them. Vasugupta says (in *Spanda Kārikā* III.19):[95] The *Spanda-tattva* consists of perfect I-consciousness. When one is firmly fixed in it and controls the *udbhava*(creation, emanation) and *laya* (absorption) of the *puryaṣṭaka* (the subtle body constituted of five *Tanmātras, Manas, Buddhi* and *Ahaṁkāra*) independently, he renounces his position of the enjoyable object (*bhojya*) and attains the status of an enjoyer (*bhoktā*) and ultimately becomes the Lord of the *cakra* (group of sense-deities). The word '*ekatra*' (in one place) is explained.[96] Everything should be deposited into one (fixed) place viz *citi-śakti.* (*Spanda* K.III.12)

Kṣema explains this: Here '*ekatra*'means the *cit* being of the nature of *unmeṣa*, in the state of vibrating *Cit*.

The word '*tasya*' in (*Spanda* K.III.19) means, according to Kṣema, 'Subtle body' (*Puryaṣṭaka*) by which he individual soul) is bound.[97]

Kṣema concludes by quoting his eulogistic verse:[98] Not being under the control of sense he who has become an independent master and who is the supreme ruler—*cakravartī* of the circle of deities governing the senses, and who is served by the group of deities presiding over senses, is an indescribable person who becomes victorious.

The word '*iti*' in the Sūtra implies 'conclusion'. The word 'Śiva' in the Sūtra means, whatever has been stated in this text is Śiva, as it has been propagated (*prasṛta*) by Śiva. It is not different from the real nature of Śiva. It is indeed Śiva Himself.

Here ends the text of Pratyabhijñā-hṛdaya.

Additional verses by Kṣemarāja.

Kṣemarāja's Concluding Remarks[99]

One does not recognize one's own *Citi* (consciousness) which is of the nature of Maheśvara and is (as if a) compact of complete bliss as he is restricted continuously by all (activities or phases) of waking, dream, sleep by the body, Prāṇa, pleasure, etc.

But he is spoken of as Śiva himself who due to the advice tendered here (in this book) discerned in the ocean of nectarine spiritual (awareness that the universe is a mass of the foam of nectarine awareness on all sides).

The last verse is the repetition of the opening paragraph of this book which mentions for whom the present work is written:

"To them who for want of discipline of serious study of Śāstras are not competent to understand *Īśvara-Pratyabhijñā* that the *Pratyabhijñā* doctrine of Utpalācārya but on whom the *śaktipāta* (Descent of Śakti) has been conferred by Lord Śiva."[100]

Concluded is this *Pratyabhijñā-hṛdaya* colophon:

This book is by the famous teacher Rājānaka Kṣemarāja who depends on the lotus-feet of glorious Abhinavagupta—a great Śaiva teacher.

May there be auspiciousness to all.

Chapter 5

Mādhavācārya on *Pratyabhijñā* Philosophy

Mādhavācārya who later ascended the *pīṭha* of Śaṅkarācārya at Śṛṅgeri (Karnataka) was the spiritual guide of Harihara and Bukka, the founders of Vijayanagar Kingdom. He was a very great scholar who richly contributed to Vedānta. He wanted to show how his *Kevalādvaita* view on Vedānta is correct. He reviewed (and criticised) the philosophy of different schools current at his time including that of Bṛhaspati (Cārvāka), non-Vedic schools like Jainism and Vedic schools of Śaiva, Vaiṣṇava and Śākta persuasion.

After considering (and evaluating) the Śaiva Schools of Nakulīśa (*Pāśupata-darśana*) and 'Śaiva *darśana* i.e. Siddhānta Śaivism, he reviews *Īśvarādvayavāda* that is Kashmir Śaivism, especially its branch called *Pratyabhijñā*. The title '*Pratyabhijñā-darśana*' which I adopted for the present work, is originally Mādhavācārya's title of the review of the *Pratyabhijñā* doctrine.

For the sake of authoritative presentation of this doctrine, Mādhavācārya adopted passages after passages, from Utpala's *Īśvara-Pratyabhijñā* and its *Vimarśinī* commentary by Abhinavagupta.

Pratyabhijñā Darśana

(A free translation)

Insentients have no causal capacity. But the previous Śaiva (i.e. *Siddhānta Śaiva*) schools regard it as a cause. But persons who thereby regard it as invalid, accept another philosophical position. They proclaim that the creation of the universe is solely due to the will of God. They believe that Maheśvara has absolute sovereignty of will or free will. He can do anything like the creation, maintenance etc. of the universe with His free-will-power without the help of external material or instruments. He need not at all look (with any expectation) to others (for help etc.) (*ananya-mukha-prekṣitva*). His identity with individual soul is proved both by Āgama and self-knowledge (*Saṁvedana*). Maheśvara is like a mirror. In that mirror, He shows the reflections of all objects.

The school which holds these views is called *Pratyabhijñā*. This (path of) *Pratyabhijñā* is easy for adoption to all. No internal or external exertions like *caryā, Prāṇāyāma* etc. are required in this school. Such is the nature of the *Pratyabhijñā* School.

Authoritative Works

In a Kārikā[1], Mādhava (ācārya) notes the following works which are the fundamental treatises on *Pratyabhijñā-darśana*. They are: Utpalācārya's: (1) *Sūtra (Īśvara-Pratyabhijñā-Sūtra* i.e. the *Kārikās),* (2) *Pratyabhijñā Vṛtti,* (3) *Pratyabhijñā-Vivṛti* and Abhinavagupta's, (4) *Pratyabhijñā-Vimarśinī,* and (5) *Pratyabhijñā-Vivṛti-Vimarśinī.* To us (3) is not extant and hence (5) its commentary, is not much useful. It appears Mādhava must have with him all these five books (MSS). We have already discussed this is the Introduction in Chapter 1.

After stating the sources of this information about *Pratyabhijñā* Mādhava proceeds to delineate what he understood by the doctrine of *Pratyabhijñā.* Mādhava quotes the first Sūtra of I.P.I-I and explains it, quoting verbatim the commentary of Abhinava as follows:

I. After anyhow (inexplicably) realizing my identity with the Supreme Lord (Maheśvara), I wish to render service to mankind. With this aim in view, I establish *Pratyabhijñā* doctrine as that alone is the means (path) of attaining *Mokṣa* (literally the most valued), Mādhava explains practically every word of this verse as per Abhi's commentary:

Kathañcit—The spiritual preceptor is the Supreme Lord incarnate. By properly propitiating the lotus-feet of the preceptor, by the grace of God.
Āsādya—*Ā*—on all sides, completely, thoroughly.
Sādayitvā—'making him (the disciple) unobstructedly competent for self-realization by his own efforts. Thus because of his having known the knowable (*vidita-vedya*) his competence to present this *Pratyabhijñā* system for others is shown. If he be not so (viz. *viditavedya*), he would be a sheer impostor.
Maheśvara—Powerful gods like Viṣṇu, Viriñci (Brahmā) who

have crossed Māyā, but are within the sphere of Mahāmāyā. But it is by the sparks of this power that they have attained Godhead. His essential nature is perfect Freedom which consists of unbroken self-refulgence and self-consciousness (such is Maheśvara).

Dāsya—A state of devotee all whose desires (wants) are fulfilled by the Lord. Thus *'dāsa'* means one who is competent to receive the perfect Will-power of the Lord which is not different from Maheśvara.

Jana—An ordinary person (lit. anyone who is born). There is no restriction regarding the eligibility to enter the path of *Pratyabhijñā*. Whosoever realizes the true nature of the self attains the highest goal. There is no impediment.

The great-grand-teacher, Somānanda has said in the *Śiva-dṛṣṭi*[3]:

"When one gets firm, clear knowledge of Śiva's omnipresence, through the means of right knowledge, scriptures or guru's guidance, the instruments of knowledge and meditation become perfectly superfluous. For once gold is known as such, are instruments necessary to reveal its genuineness? The certainty is like the firm belief, as in one's parents."

Janasya: Jana: Ordinary person always troubled by the cycle of births and deaths.

Api: The word shows our identity with God. It precludes any other motive except the good of others.

The good of others can be a real motive because the definition of motive applies to it. God had not cursed that only one's own good can become a motive and not that of others. Hence *Akṣapāda* defined motive as that aiming at which man acts (*Gautama Sūtra* I.1.24).

Upapādayāmi: The preposition—*upa*—in 'upakāra' shows 'vicinity', 'nearness'. It indicates bringing of men near God. Hence, he has called *Pratyabhijñā* 'the cause of attaining all covetables' (*samasta-sampad-samavāpti-hetu*). The aim here is to bring ordinary men nearer the state of the Highest Reality. Once that stage is reached all attainable things which flow from it are automatically attained just as all precious stones are acquired when the mountain of gems, Rohaṇa, is acquired. What has remained for which prayer is to be extended?

Utpalācārya says:[4]

"Those who are rich in the wealth of devotion to the Lord, have nothing left to be desired. But those who are lacking it, what is the use of coveting other things?"

The above interpretation is when we take *samastavastu* as a genitive compound.

Another interpretation

If we dissolve that compound as Bahuvrīhi (attributive compound), the means are shown : That is the recognition of the Highest Reality (*Pratyabhijñā*) in which (*yasyām*), clear consciousness (*samavāpti*) of the essential nature (*sampat*) of an external and internal object both existing and non-existing. Such as 'blue' (external object), 'pleasure' (mental i.e. internal object) etc. (*samasta*) is the cause (*hetu*) internal—(Based on Dr. K.C. Pandey).

Samastasya: The attainment of the true self is possible only through an investigation of the ultimate source of the knowledge of external objects (such as 'blue') and internal objects (such as 'pleasure') which affect so distinctly the consciousness. In other words: Maheśvara was (anyhow) forgotten. *Pratyabhijñā* is knowledge of Maheśvara (as facing oneself).[5]

In practical life, recognition consists of the unification of what appeared once with what appeared now, as in the judgement "this is the same (man called) Caitra". It is cognition of the object which is directly present. 'Recognition' means shining (*Jña-jñana*) as facing oneself (*ābhimukhyena*) of what was forgotten. *Pratiparn* implies that it is not that the consciousness of the Self has never before been a fact of experience, because it always shines. Recognition consists in the unification of experiences at the time of the subsequent apprehension of one who was known before.

The knowledge of the Lord as endowed with Supreme Power is known through Purāṇas, Āgamas, Siddhānta and inference. There is the immediate apprehension of one's own self as being these. Recognition arises through the unification of these two experiences that 'I am that very Lord, I shall establish that recognition'.

Objection

If the self is essentially of the same nature as that of the Lord, what need is there to establish the realization of *Pratyabhijñā*. *Reply*: True. The self-being, self-luminous, is ever-shining, but due to Māyā his light is greatly obstructed and only a part of it reaches out. In order to get thorough knowledge of the soul, the powers of knowledge and action must be exercised.

The syllogistic statement about this is as follows:

(i) The self deserves to be the Lord.
(ii) For he possesses the powers of knowledge and action.
(iii) He who possesses the powers of knowledge and action is Īśvara to that extent. e.g. a king.
(iv) The self is the knower and maker of the whole universe.
(v) Therefore, the self is Īśvara.
Following Maheśvara, the *Pratyabhijñā*-vādins accept the five steps of this syllogism of the followers of Nyāya and Māyāvādins accept it.

After this introductory discussion, Mādhava quotes *Īśvara-Pratyabhijñā* (I.1.1).[6] It states: "Maheśvara is omnipotent and omnipresent. He is eternal. What sentient being—man— can prove or disprove the Supreme Lord. (He means that if a thing is unproved, you can prove or disprove it. But a self-existing entity, God, can neither be proved nor disproved)."

In support of this, *Mādhava quotes*[7] *(IPI.1.2, 3 and 4)*

"But even though He be seen [is known] all his powers are obscured by Māyā. Hence they cannot be fully experienced or realized. But by the manifestation of these powers of knowledge and action of the soul, it helps to bring about the recognition of the soul and nothing else." (IPI12).

"Similarly the very existence of insentients completely depends on the sentients. The powers of knowledge and action are the very life of the sentients." (IPI.1.3)

"Of these (two) the power of knowledge as also the power of action, are self-established. Power when associated with the body is perceptible by other limited perceivers. From that the presence of the powers of knowledge in others is guessed." (IP.V.1.14)

Here, ends the 1st *Adhikaraṇa* of *Jñānādhikāra*.

The consciousness, which shines affected by a succession of variety of objects (*literally* and this consciousness of the object) is nothing but the great Lord (Maheśvara), the subject. Essentially, he is the eternal and unchanging light of consciousness.[8]

The great teacher Somānanda has said: "Sadāśiva knows as myself. And I know as Sadāśiva." [vide I.1.4 for further explanation of this observation of Somānanda]. In concluding the section *Jñānādhikāra* in *Īśvara-pratyabhijñā* (I.8, 10-11)[9] he says:

> "Therefore, without the unification of *saṁvids* (cognitions), no worldly transaction is possible. They are unified because of oneness of the light (of consciousness). And that light is the one subject. This is established. And that very one subject is the Highest Lord, because, he is everfree and because this freedom is identical with the independent powers of knowledge and action of the playful Lord."

Abhinava explains (these Kārikas): Without the unification of cognitions (*saṁvids*) worldly transactions are impossible. Their possibility is a proof of their unification. This is not difficult to establish. For the light that illuminates the objects (*viṣaya-prakāśa*) is spoken of as the light of consciousness. Due to the affection of light of consciousness by the objects (and due to its extroversion) the light illuminating a *nīla* object (appears) different. In reality however light of consciousness, being free from the limitation of time, place and form, is the only one. That is spoken of as the subject.

In *Śiva-Sūtra* it is stated: "Ātman (the self) is *Caitanya*. Its synonyms are: *cid-rūpatva* (being consciousness in form), *anavacchinna-vimarśatva* (whose being Vimarśa or being a doer is eternal), *ananyon-mukha* (having no need to look to others for help etc.), *svatantrya* (full freedom), *ānanda-ghanatva* (being as if a compact of bliss). Knowledge of reality and action is His (Ātman) *Vimarśa*. His knowledge is His luminosity, and creation of the universe from himself is His action."

Utpala in *Kriyādhikāra* section of IP (II. 4.1) *says*[10]:

> "The Lord is of unlimited powers. He makes the objects manifest through His will-power. It is this power of action in which consists His creativeness."[10]

In concluding, the *Kriyādhikāra* of IP, *Utpala says:*

> "Thus the Will itself of the Lord who will (has the desire)

to appear as (objects such as) jar and cloth etc., which constitute the world—which is nothing but an Ābhāsa—is the cause, the agent and the action."[11]

Abhinava explains: [Mādhava does not include this] "Action is the strange will of the Lord. He is free. He wills to appear in the form of the universe constituted by Ābhāsas of jar etc. in the various stages of their becoming such as creation, existence etc. and thousands of their sub-varieties. Hence, the glorious Highest Lord alone is the creator of the universe."

If this be the case the causal relation is in the sentients. Insentients are devoid of any expectation. Hence, the causal relation is not applicable to insentients.[12]

In the same way, inasmuch as insentients cannot be a cause (*lit.* if causality is not inherent in the insentients), it is not inherent in the sentient who is not *Īśvara* (master or Lord). In the world, thousands of differences and action are found/seen in the stages of births (creation), maintenance and in *vikāras* (changes). Maheśvara desires to abide in those forms. This free will manifesting itself in these (and such) objects is called the creativity of the universe. The instance (example) of the creation of the world by sheer will-power is already given.

As Utpala says in IP II.4.10

"By sheer power of will of the Yogins, even without clay and seeds etc., which have permanency and serve their respective purposes, come into being."[13]

Objection

If clay etc. be the real cause of objects like jar *etc.* how is it possible that jars etc. are created merely by the will-power of Yogins.

Abhinava explains: As a rule objects like jar etc. are not created without any material cause (like clay). It is not correct to say that a Yogin sees the necessary atoms and brings them together by His will-power. Causal laws are not violated even in the creation of a Yogin. Thus in the case of a jar, clay, wheel and rod, etc. and in that of (human) body cohabitation of man and woman and lapse of the necessary long period for the production of the effect will be necessary.

Thus the creation of jar and body etc. by a Yogin's will-power will be difficult to establish.

But there is no plan (in Yogin's creativity by will-power). Mahādeva, the sentient Lord of great glory, is perfectly free to follow or transgress the laws of *Niyati.*

Hence, *Vasuguptācārya in paying obeisance to Śiva says:* "I bow that Śiva, who is praiseworthy, because of Kalā. He paints the picture of the world on 'no wall'. (*abhittau*) without the multitude of material causes."[14]

Objection

If individual soul (*Pratyagātmā* or *Pramātā*) is not different from the Supreme Lord, how is it that He is related (gets bound in *saṁsāra*)?

Utpala replies[15]: As he is blinded by Māyā the subject (individual soul, *Pramātā*) is limited by time etc. He thinks that he is bound by Karmas and is transmigratory. But when he is made to recognise his powers by true knowledge and as he is pure *cit* (consciousness), he is spoken of as liberated.

Objection

If it be a fact that there is no difference between 'the things to be measured', the means of valid knowledge and the *Pramātā* (individual soul) what is the difference between the liberated soul and the soul in bondage in relation to the objects.

Utpala replies[16]: The liberated one looks upon the common object as one with himself (*svātmābhedena*) as does Maheśvara, the great Lord. But the one who is bound sees it (a common object) as altogether different from himself. [I may add Abhinava's commentary on this verse: The liberated one thinks: All that can be the object of cognition of any being in the universe is also of mine and similarly my object of cognition is that of all beings in the universe.]

Doubt

If the individual soul is inherently the great Lord and if the essential nature of the self is ever the same, then there would be no difference in its causal efficiency (*arthakriyā*) in the case of its recognition or non-recognition. *Pratyabhijñā* is superfluous. For a seed may not be recognized. But if its contributory causes of growth (suitable soil, water, manure, etc.) are present, the unrecognized seed produces the sprout. Why then is such an emphasis on self-recognition?

The Reply

You see, the causal efficiency is of two types: (i) External, such as the production of the sprout and (ii) Internal, such as causing pleasure etc. It is essentially nothing else than the self-consciousness, the rest or relaxation of the subject on itself.

(1) the former undoubtedly does not require recognition but the latter, and (2) does stand in need of recognition. Here, in this case the causal efficiency lies in the arousal of the consciousness: "I am the Highest Lord". This consciousness is characterised by the possession (by the realiser) of both higher and lower Siddhis and the glories of the liberated in the life.

In this case, *Pratyabhijñā* is absolutely necessary.

Doubt

Where do you find that the causal efficiency which is essentially rest (*viśrānti*) on the subject, is not seen without *Pratyabhijñā* and is co-incidental with the same (recognition)?

Utpala replies giving a romantic illustration:[17] Before translating the verse, the background is narrated for clear understanding of the doctrine of *Pratyabhijñā.* On hearing the excellent qualities etc. of a young man (hero), passion of love was aroused in a young lady. Day and night she intensely desired to see him. Her heart got out of control. She began to send him messengers, write love letters presenting her lovelorn condition. She became slimmer by the pangs of separation. Lo and behold! The hero in response to her earnest requests, unexpectedly comes to her and stands before her. But she was not able to apprehend his distinctive great qualities which attracted her. So he was nothing more than an ordinary man to her. Similarly, though the Lord of the universe is ever shining within as the very self, yet His brilliance (shining) does not fill the heart with bliss (*Ānanda*). For the self is not realized to be transcendental and preserving the supreme Lordliness which is unchecked by freedom of thought and action. Thus the self is (to the ignorant) an ordinary object like a jar etc.

But in the case of that lovelorn lady, her heart bloomed fully like a wonderful bud when her friend or a messenger pointed out to her that he is her real object of Love and has the excellences and characteristics that she loved, she got united with him and got repeated enjoyment of union and perfect rest in the heart.

Similarly either as a result of one's preceptor's guidance or recognition of His powers or actions, he immediately, within his life time gets final liberation characterised by perfection.

Thus it is the recognition of the self which gives both the higher and lower spiritual power.

The verse mentioned above may be translated as follows:

'Just as an object of Love, who has been brought to the presence of the slim lady by her previous entreaties, cannot give her any pleasure, though he may stand before her, so long as he is not recognised and therefore not distinguished from common man; so the self of all, which is the Lord of the world, cannot manifest its true glory so long as its essential nature is not recognised.'

Hence the means of recognition has been dealt with—Pandey

Teachers like Abhinavagupta and others have explained this theory in details. We (Mādhava) did not discuss in details as we have to make a brief statement of the doctrine.

Chapter 6

Epilogue

We have seen that *Pratyabhijñā* is a path to Śiva—realization or *Mokṣa*. So were *Upāyas*—Śāṁbhava, Śākta and Āṇava—enunciated in the *Śiva Sūtra* by Vasugupta. Somānanda, a disciple of Vasugupta, studied ancient scriptures and came to the conclusion that Śivahood is a very exalted state of mind. It is rather a psychological process which leads one to the highest spiritual status. If that be the case, what is the propriety of external physical exertions involved in Yogic exercises like *Prāṇāyāma, Bandha* etc. Some methods which calm down the mind and help concentration or developing deep conviction of one's being Śiva Himself, will be easier to ordinary householders while carrying out their worldly responsibilities. It was a revolutionary departure from the Upāyas advised by his teacher Vasugupta.

It was, however, left to Somānanda's disciple Utpaladeva to formulate it systematically in *Īśvara-Pratyabhijñā*. He declares his path as 'easy and new'.

sughaṭa eṣa mārgo navo

But the pathway was not altogether 'new'. Maybe for emphasizing the authenticity of *Pratyabhijñā* as a path to *Mokṣa*, Utpala quotes the authority of his great-grand-teacher's work *Śivadṛṣṭi*. Utpala's disciple, the colossal polymath Abhinavagupta brought out the full significance of the doctrine though he assumed the low profile as a commentator of *Īśvara-Pratyabhijñā*.

Curiously enough, Kṣemarāja, an eminent disciple of Abhinava, adopted a catholicity of outlook and regarded the fundamental doctrines of rival schools of philosophy such as Cārvākas, Naiyāyikas, Bauddhas, Vedāntins *et al* as various actor-like 'parts' assumed by the soul (P.Ḥ. Sūtra 8). In advising paths to Śivahood or *Mokṣa*, he does not limit himself to the paths prescribed in

Pratyabhijñā but includes the non-*Pratyabhijñā* methods[1] also, as they too have the authority of sacred traditions (*āmnāyikatvāt*).

Paths to Śivahood

Dissolution of Vikalpas

Our mind is never calm and quiet. It is always ruffled with different thoughts, ideas, perceptions, fancies etc. These movements disturbing the peace or quiet condition of the mind are called *Vikalpas*. They present obstacles while concentrating the mind on Śiva.

1. Vikalpa-Kṣaya

For controlling *Vikalpas*, Kṣema advises to meditate on the five actions (*Pañcakṛtyas*) of Śiva and of Jiva's doing the same in his own way. Kṣema, on P.H. Sūtra 10 says: "Those who ponder over the five-fold activity of the Lord become liberated in this very life"[2] (as they experience gradually their identity with Śiva). Abhinava on IP.IV 1. 11 explains a procedure of *Vikalpa-kṣaya*. But it is rather Yogic.

At first one should concentrate one's attention on an external object. Gradually he should try to meditate to himself that 'the external object or the world is I myself — nothing is different from me.' Thus one's identity with the world at large gradually gets established'.

He however advises further to practice *Śāṁbhavī Mudrā* in which one has to keep one's eyes wide open without winking, but the mind is concentrated within. By the practice of this *Mudrā* and by the 'world assimilating' meditation, *Vikalpas* get dissolved and Parama Śiva is realized and one attains *Mokṣa* while alive.

As Vasugupta says; "With the subsidence of mutual agitation, Divinity emerges (Spandakārikā I.9). Kṣema gives topmost priority to this *Pratyabhijñā* method of attaining Śivahood".

This method resembles *Vipaśyanā* to some extent.

2. Sóham

Utpala and Abhinava were aware of the impossibility of complete elimination of *Vikalpas*. They advised another procedure:

One should try to get the following consciousness firmly established. "I am not different from the Supreme Self. That transcendental Being I am, and He is I". All *Vikalpas* are my creation, my own glory, my power of freedom."[3]

When this consciousness becomes firmly established, man becomes liberated immediately during his life-time, even though *Vikalpas* are not completely dissolved.

This method is similar to the Vedāntic method of meditation: "I am definitely Śiva, consciousness and bliss incarnate."[4]

Kṣema has given some other methods — some Yogic, some esoteric. It is with the help of books on Yoga that I tried to explain them in my translation and notes. Readers are advised *not* to practice them unless under the guidance of a competent *guru.*

The following are the additional methods given by Kṣema in P.H. in Sūtra 17:

(1) Development of the Madhya (*Suṣumṇā Nāḍī*).
(2) *Saṅkoca* and *Vikāsa* (contraction and development) of Śakti.
(3) Cutting of *Vāhas* (a special method of *Prāṇāyāma*).
(4) Practice of noting or concentrating on the extreme (starting) points of inhalation and exhalation (*ādyanta-koṭi-nibhālana*).

The ultimate aim is to secure concentration of mind on Parama Śiva and realize one's identity with Him through Recognition. Maybe by Śiva-realization one could feel (or experience) that the universe is a part of one's own self and vice-versa. What is the positive gain (not in material wealth) from psychological point of view? Kṣema in the last Sūtra of *Pratybhijñā-Hṛdayam* 20 enumerates: gain as essence of *Cit* (consciousness) and bliss, power over all *Mantras,* Lordship over the deities who create and dissolve the universe as a result of *Samādhilābha.* It is a stage of liberation from *Saṁsāra* during one's life-time, attainment of infinite power and bliss both during *Samādhi* and *Post-Samādhi* period.

What more can an aspirant for *Mokṣa* expect? And it is to an ordinary person (untrained in disciplines of *Nyāya* etc.) to whom *Pratyabhijñā* is addressed.

Relevance of Pratyabhijñā today

The *Pratyabhijñā* ideal of Śiva-realization and the practice of *Vikalpa-kṣaya* and a sort of hypnotizing oneself in Śivahood may be all right in the care of those who have taken to spiritual path.

Materialism, atheism, scepticism and agnosticism shall continue to dominate human mind as they do it today. Indulgence in externalities, sensuous objects, in physical pleasure shall continue to drive people to cut-throat competition resulting in mental tensions, psycho-somatic troubles, heart disease and the like. Drugs or Psychiatry cannot provide effective remedies on these sufferings. *Pratyabhijñā* philosophy and practices are based on psychology and as such will be found to be a soothing factor if not a panacea to the suffering humanity.

Pratyabhijñā declares that every human being is essentially Supreme Śiva, No Māyā or Fate can obstruct your way to Śiva-recognition and ultimate absorption into Parama Śiva. This declaration kindles strong hope in all — especially the down-trodden and unfortunate people. It is a sort of elixir to negative thinkers who torment themselves with imaginary fears.

It is true that the pathways to Śiva-realization are primarily meant for people who have taken to spiritual way of life. But Somānanda and disciples have prescribed these for householders who will find Yoga and Vasugupta's Upāyas as incompatible with their domestic responsibilities. Hence these practices will certainly prove useful even to ambitious, successful careerists who suffer from insomnia and allied ailments. The practice prescribed is simple. *Vikalpa-kṣaya* is similar to *Vipaśyanā* which has now become so popular. Self-identification with Śiva is the age-old practice among Vedāntins whose *japa* is 'I am He' (*so'ham*). No *guru* except one's own self is required for these practices. Those who practice these regularly will find that they have improved in their efficiency in their professions, vocations and even social and home life. *Pratyabhijñā* echoes Kṛṣṇa's words: "Meditate on me and fight".

Notes

Introduction

1. This is corroborated by Varadarāja, the commentator on Vasugupta's *Śiva Sūtra.* In the introductory verse of his *Vārtika* (commentary) on *Śiva Sūtra,* he says:
   नागबोध्यादिभिः सिद्‌धैर्नास्तिकानां पुरःसरैः ।
   आक्रान्ते जीवलोकेऽस्मिन् आत्मेश्वर-निरासकैः ।। —शि.सू. वार्त्तिक
2. Kalhaṇa records:
   क्रियां नीलपुराणोक्ताम् आच्छिन्दन् आगमद्विषः ।—राजतरंगिणी I. 178
3. Thus we find Purāṇic statements like the following
   (i) बद्धो नवमको जातो ।—मत्स्यपुराण 47.247
   (ii) तथा बुद्धत्वमपरं नवमं प्राप्स्यतेऽच्युत ।—स्कन्द-रेवाखण्ड 151.21
4. The present belief that Śaṅkara *lived* in the 8th century A.D. is based on an unauthenticated *MS.* discovered by K.B. Pathak at Belgaum in the nineteenth century. But now the date deserves reconsideration as Bhāvaviveka, a Buddhist Philosopher (490-500 A.D.) quotes as *Pūrvapakṣa Kārikās* from Gauḍapāda's *Māṇḍūkya Kārikās.* That means we must locate Gauḍapāda earlier than Bhāvaviveka as he found Gauḍapāda an important author deserving refutation. This implies that Gauḍapāda must have lived by *circa* 500 A.D.
   Śaṅkara was the disciple of Govinda Yati, the disciple of Gauḍapāda. Now if we presume that a generation means a period of 30 years, Śaṅkara is removed from Gauḍapāda by two generations that is about 60 years. Thus Śaṅkara must be located in the 6th century A.D.

Chapter 1

1. Teachers of the *Pratyabhijñā* Doctrine
   Śaṅkara mentions this number in the stotra Saundarya-Laharī as follows:
   चतुःष्टया तन्त्रैः सकलमभिसंधा.....
2. कदाचिद् असौ (=शिवः) 'द्वैत-दर्शनाधिवासितप्राये
   जीवलोके रहस्य-संप्रदायो (ईश्वराद्वयवाद) मा
   विच्छेदि' इत्याशयतः.....परमशिवेन (वसुगुप्तः)
   स्वप्ने अनुगृह्य उन्मिषितप्रतिभः कृतः यथा 'अत्र
   महीभृति महति शिलातले रहस्यं अस्ति तद् अधिगम्य
   अनुग्रहयोग्येषु प्रकाशय' इति ।—क्षेमराज, शिवसूत्रप्रस्तावना
   This inscribed slab is untraceable
3. Kallaṭa in concluding his commentary on *Spanda Kārikā,* confirms that

Vasugupta is the author of the Kārikā and he is only a commentator. States Kallaṭa:

दृब्धं महादेव-गिरौ महेश-स्वप्नोपदिष्टात् शिवसूत्र-सिन्धोः।
स्पन्दामृतं यद् वसुगुप्त-पादैः श्रीकल्लटः तत् प्रकटीचकार॥

4. Śivadṛṣṭi VII. 112-113
Durvāsas named his mental son 'Tryaṁbaka' after the cave, his birthplace
5. स च कालेन कश्मीरेष्वागतो भ्रमन्। op. cit., VII. 118
6. op. cit., VII. 119-120
7. सुघट एष मार्गो नवः। Īśvara-Pratyabhijñā-Vimarśinī IV. 1-16
8. प्रतिपादितमेतावत् (views expressed in शिवदृष्टि)
सर्वमेव शिवात्मकम्।
न स्वबुद्धया शिवो दाता शिवो भोक्तेति शास्त्रतः। —Śivadṛṣṭi, VII.105-106
9. These are the benedictory verses:
अस्मद् रूपसमाविष्टः स्वात्मनात्मनिवारणे।
शिवः करोतु निजया नभः शक्त्या ततात्मने।।
आत्मैव सर्वभावेषु स्फुरन् निर्वृतचिद् विभुः।
अनिरुद्धेच्छा-प्रसरः प्रसरद् दृक्-क्रियः शिवः।। —Śivadṛṣṭi I. 1-2
10. इत्याहुस्ते परं ब्रह्म यदनादि तथाक्षयम्।
तदक्षरं शब्दरूपं सा पश्यन्ती परा हि वाक् ।। op. cit., II. 2
11. यथा सर्वपदार्थानां भगवच्छिवरूपता।
तद्वद् वागिन्द्रियस्यापि, न पुनः सा परा दशा।। op. cit., II 88
12. भेदे हि शक्तिः किं कार्यं करोत्युत च शक्तिमान्।
शक्तेः स्वातन्त्र्यकार्यत्वात् शिवत्वं न क्वचिद् भवेत्।। op. cit., III. 5-6
13. न हिमस्य पृथक् शैत्यं नाग्नेरौष्ण्यं पृथक् भवेत्...
तस्मात् समग्राकारेषु सर्वासु प्रतिपत्तिषु।
विज्ञेयं शिवरूपत्वम्.... op. cit., III. 7-17
14. op. cit., III. 21-28
15. op. cit., III. 36-39
16. Utpala, the commentator, explains verse 96-97:
चिद्द्रयस्य देश-काल-स्वभावभेदाभावात् न भेदः
एतद् ईश्वरप्रत्यभिज्ञायां प्रदर्शितम्।
17. घटचितस्तावन्मात्ररूपाया स्वातन्त्र्ये पट-चिता सह
अनुसन्धानं न स्यात्। तस्मादेकमेव चित्तत्वं अनन्तविश्व-
रूपम्।—उत्पल on VV. 3-5
18. तस्माद् ऐक्यमिह स्पष्टं संसारे समवस्थितम्।
परस्परेण चाप्यत्र तेषां रूपेण वाऽन्यथा।
तस्मात् समस्तभावानामैक्येनैवास्ति संगमः।। op. cit., IV. 122-123
19. सर्वेभावाः स्वमात्मानं जानन्तः सर्वतः स्थिताः।
मदात्मना घटो वेत्ति वेद्म्यहं घटात्मना।।
सदाशिवात्मना वेत्ति स वा वेत्ति मदात्मना।। 1064
मद्रूपत्वं घटस्यास्ति ममास्ति घटरूपता।। 1084

एवं सर्वेषु भावेषु सर्वसाम्ये व्यवस्थिते।
तेन सर्वगतं सर्वं शिवरूपं निरूपितम्।। 110 op. cit., V. 105-110

20. तद् भूमिका: सर्वदर्शनस्थितय:। —प्रत्यभिज्ञाहृदय सूत्र 8
"The positions taken by all schools of philosophy are the various roles of the Ātman or consciousness"

21. Later writers like Utpala and others have freely quoted many verses from this chapter. For example:
सकृज्ज्ञाते सुवर्णे हि भावना करणं व्रजेत्।
एकवारं प्रमाणेन शास्त्राद् वा गुरूवाक्यत:॥ 5॥
ज्ञाते शिवत्वे सर्वस्थे प्रतिपत्त्या दृढात्मन:।
करणेन नास्तिकृत्यं क्वापि भावनयाऽपिवा॥ 6॥

22. शिवोऽस्मीति मनोह्लादो जलस्नानं पर मतम् VII. 89 A
सर्वाभावा: शिवाकारा अन्तर्भूता शिवानले।
सोऽहं शिव: सुतृप्तोऽस्मि होम इत्युदित: पर:॥ 91 VII
लिंगादिके पूजितोऽस्मि सदा पूजेति वा स्थित:।
पूजक: पूजनं पूज्यं इति सर्वं शिवं स्थित:॥ VII. 94
शिवो भोक्ता शिवो भोज्यं शिवेषु शिवसाधन:॥ VII. 99
शिव: कर्ता शिव: कर्म शिवोऽस्मि करणात्मक:॥ VII. 100
सुखे दु:खे विमोहे च स्थितोऽहं परम: शिव:।
प्रतिपादितमेतावत् सर्वमेव शिवात्मकम्॥ VII. 105

23. इति कथितमशेषं शैवरूपेण विश्वं
जगदुदित महेशांघ्र्या(घ्रि+आ)ज्ञया स्वप्नभाजा।
यदधिगमबलेन प्राप्य सम्यग् विकासं
भवति शिवमयात्मा सर्वभावेन सर्व: ॥ VII. 106

24. तदेवमेतद् विहितं मया प्रकरणं मनाक् । VII. 122
प्राश्र्यन्तेऽस्मिन् प्रयुक्तेऽपि गुरवो ग्रहणं प्रति॥

25. Utpaladeva, the disciple of Somānanda, has adopted this concept of *Śiva* in *toto* in *Īśvara-pratyabhijñā*

26. सुघट एष मार्गो नवो। IPV IV. 1-16

27. जनस्यायत्नसिद्ध्यर्थं उदयाकरसूनुना।
ईश्वरप्रत्यभिज्ञेयं उत्पलेन उपपादिता॥ IPV IV.18

28. सूत्रं वृत्तिर्विवृतिर्लघ्वीबृहतीत्युभे विमर्शिन्यौ।
प्रकरण-विवरण-पञ्चकमिति शास्त्रं प्रत्यभिज्ञाया:। —सर्वदर्शनसंग्रह-प्रत्यभिज्ञादर्शन
Abhinava wrote commentaries both on Utpala's *Vṛtti* on his work *Īśvara-pratyabhijñā.* It was a short work and hence is called लघ्वी(laghvī) विमर्शिनी The *Vivṛti* was a bigger work and is mentioned in the above work as बृहती.

29. In explaining आसाद्य in IP. I. 1-1, Abhinava remarks: "The writer of the *Vṛtti* (i.e. Utpala) did not explain this as his object was simply to express the implication of the *Vṛtti*"
(इयति च व्याख्याने वृत्तिकृता (उत्पलेन) भरो न कृत:। तात्पर्यव्याख्यानात्। यदुक्तं-संवृत-सौत्र-निर्देश विवृतिमात्र व्यापारायाम्) —ई. प्र. वृ. IP. 39

30. Abhinava proudly mentions his father as follows:
तस्य (वराहगुप्तस्य) आत्मजः चुखुलकेति जने प्रसिद्धः।
चन्द्रावदातधिषणो नरसिंहगुप्तः॥
यं सर्वशास्त्ररसमज्जनशुभ्रचित्तम्
माहेश्वरी परमलंकुरुते स्म भक्तिः॥ —तंत्रालोक आ. 37
31. K. C. Pandey. *Abhinavagupta* pp. 10-11
32. op. cit. pp. 22-23. For contents of his works see pp. 24-67
33. कृतिः तत्रभवन् महामाहेश्वराचार्यवर्य-श्रीमद् अभिनवगुप्तपाद-
पद्मोप-जीविनः श्रीमतो राजानकक्षेमाचार्यस्य।
34. K. C. Pandey, *Abhinavagupta* p. 156

Chapter 2

1. तच्च (त्रिकशास्त्रम्) सिद्धा-नामक-मालिनी-आख्य-खण्डत्रयात्मकत्वात् त्रिविधम्।
—तंत्रालोक I. 45
2. तदेवं परं त्रिकं परामृश्य परापरमपि परामृष्टमाह। —तंत्रालोक I. 20
3. त्रिकं सर्वोत्तमं परम्। —परात्रिंशिका-विवरण p. 62
4. For a list see Abhinavagupta (*An Historical and Philosophical Study.*—K.C. Pandey) pp. 77-87
5. For details: G.V. Tagare—Spanda Kārikā (Marathi)
6. स्पन्दनं च किञ्चित् चलनम्। एषैव च किञ्चिद् रूपता
यत् अचलमपि चलं भासते। प्रकाश-स्वरूपं नाति-
रिच्यते, अतिरिच्यते इव इति तद् अचलमेव
आभासभेदयुक्तमिव च भाति। ई.प्र. pp. 256-257
7. श्रीमत् परमशिवस्य पुनः विश्वोत्तीर्ण-विश्वात्मक-परमानन्द-
मय-प्रकाशैकघनस्य एवंविधमेव शिवादि-धरण्यन्त-
मखिलमभेदेनैव स्फुरति, न तु अन्यत् किञ्चित् ग्राह्यं वा ग्राहकं वा;
अपि तु परमशिवभट्टारकः एव इत्थं नाना-वैचित्र्य-सहस्रैः स्फुरति।
प्रत्यभिज्ञा-हृदय सूत्र.3
8. यदि निर्विमर्शः स्यात्, अनीश्वरो जडश्च प्रसज्येत्त। —क्षेम-पराप्रावेशिका p. 2
9. अकृत्रिमाहं इति विस्फुरणम्। op. cit., p. 2
10. विमर्शो नाम विश्वाकारेण, विश्वप्रकाशनेन, विश्व-
संहरणेन च अकृत्रिमाहं इति विस्फुरणम्। op. cit., p. 1-2
11. पराशक्तिरूपा चितिरेव भगवत्ती शिवभट्टारिकाऽभिन्ना चितिः
.....विश्वसिद्धिहेतुः। प्र ह. I. pp. 46-47
12. न शिवः शक्तिरहितो, न शक्तिर्व्यतिरेकिणी।
शक्ति-शक्तिमतोर्भेदः शैवे जातु न वर्ण्यते॥ —शिवदृष्टि 3.2.3
13. यथा न्यग्रोधबीजस्थः शक्तिरूपो महाद्रुमः।
तथा हृदयबीजस्थं विश्वमेतच्चराचरम्॥ —क्षेम, परात्रिंशिका. (कारिका 24)
14. चितिः प्रत्यवमर्शात्मा परा वाक् स्वरसोदिता।
स्वातन्त्र्यमेतन्मुख्यं तदैश्वर्यं परमात्मनः॥ —ईप्रवि I. 5-13

15. स च प्रकाशो न परतन्त्रः, प्रकाश्यतैव पारतन्त्र्यम्।
प्रकाश्यता च प्रकाशान्तरापेक्षितैव, न च प्रकाशान्तरं किञ्चिद्
अस्ति इति स्वतन्त्रः एव प्रकाशः। —तंत्रसार, आह्निक 1, p. 6
16. तथाबुभूषु-लक्षणा।
17. स्वातन्त्र्यं नाम यथेच्छं तत्रेच्छाप्रसरस्य अविघातः। —ईप्रवि I. 5-13
18. योगिनामिच्छया यद्वत् नानारूपोपपत्तिता॥
न चास्ति साधनं किञ्चिन् मृदादीच्छां विना प्रभोः।
तथा भगवदिच्छैव तथात्वेन प्रजायते॥ —शिवदृष्टि I. 44-45
Utpalācārya explains: तथात्वेन प्रजायते
means भगवदिच्छामात्रमेव विश्वरूपं सम्पद्यते। Thereby
Vedāntic Māyāvāda is refuted
19. चिदात्मैव हि देवोन्तः स्थितमिच्छावशाद् बहिः।
योगीव निरूपादानमर्थजातं प्रकाशते।। —ईप्रवि I. 5-7
20. उत्पत्ति-स्थिति-संहार-विलय-स्थितिकारणम्।
अनुग्रहकरं देवं प्रणतार्तिविनाशनम्।। —स्वच्छन्दतंत्र (पटल) 9 (कारिका) 3
These acts of Śiva are meant for conferring
grace on beings
21. पश्यनात् पाशनात् पशवः। ....ब्रह्मादयः
तिर्यगन्ताः ते सर्वे पशवः। —पाशुपतसूत्र (पा.सू.)
22. ब्रह्माद्याः स्थावरान्ताश्च पशवः परिकीर्तिताः।
23. पाश-बद्धत्वात् पशुत्वम् । —कुमारदेव, तत्वार्थप्रकाश pp. 31-32
24. यदा स्वहृदयवर्तिनमुक्तरूपमर्थतत्वं बहिः कर्तुमुन्मुखो
भवति तदा तदा शक्तिरिति व्याह्रियते। —महेश्वरानन्द, महार्थमञ्जरी p. 40
This *unmukhatā* or *Vimarśa* is called *Īkṣaṇa*
in *Chāndogya* Upa. (6.2. 1-3): सदेव सौम्य इदमग्र आसीदेकमेवाद्वितीयम्...तदैक्षत.
बहुस्याम् प्रजायेय।
25. Parā Prāveśikā, p. 6
26. षट्त्रिंशत्तत्वसंघातः सर्वत्राप्यनुवर्तते The Commentator
Rāma Tīrtha clarifies that these Tattvas are in
Śaivāgama —एवं षट्त्रिंशत्तत्वानि शैवागमे प्रसिद्धानि।
But he differs in details as follows:
5 Mahābhūtas+5 Prāṇas+14 sense-organs (=24)
Mahat, Kāla, Pradhāna, Māyā, Vidyā
Puruṣa [=6] and Bindu, Nāda, Śakti, Śiva, Śānta, Atīta [=6]Thus 24+6+6=36.
27. This classification is based on Jaidev
Singh's Intro. to *Pratyabhijñā-hṛdayam*
28. यदयमनुत्तरमूर्तिः निजेच्छयाऽखिलमिदं जगत् स्रष्टुम्।
पस्पन्दे स स्पन्दः प्रथमः शिवतत्त्वमुच्यते तज्ज्ञैः॥ —षट्त्रिंशंत्सन्दोहकारिका V.1
29. या सा शक्तिर्जगद्धातुः कथिता समवायिनी।
इच्छात्वं तस्य सा देवी सिसृक्षोः प्रतिपद्यते॥
मालिनीविजयतन्त्र quoted in the commentary परिमल on महार्थमञ्जरी.

30. अस्य जगत्स्रष्टुमिच्छां परिगृहीतवत: परमेश्वरस्य।
प्रथम-स्पन्द एवेच्छाशक्तितत्वं, अप्रतिहतेच्छत्वात्॥ —पराप्रावेशिका pp. 6.7
31. अथास्माकं ज्ञानशक्तिर्या सदाशिवरूपता। —शिवदृष्टि 2.9
32. तत्र प्रोन्मीलितमात्र-चित्रकल्पतया 'इद्म्'
अंशस्य अस्फुटत्वात् इच्छाप्राधान्यम्, अत:स भाविन:
समस्तराशे: बहिरवबिभासायिषा [बहिर्+अवबिभा०] —लक्षण क्रीडारसिकत्वात् अनुग्रहनिरत:
तद् भूमिकां गृह्णाति। —Rajanaka's commentary on षट्त्रिंशत्संदोह (कारिका) 3
33. सदाशिवतत्वेऽहन्ताऽऽच्छादित-अस्फुटेदन्तामयं विश्वम्। —प्रह-3. 32-33
34. ईश्वरतत्त्वे स्फुटेदन्ताऽहन्ता सामानाधिकरणात्म यादृक् विश्वं ग्राह्यम्। —Ibid
35. अत्र वेद्यजातस्य स्फुटावभासनात् ज्ञानशक्तेरुद्रेक:।
राजानक आनंद in विवरण on.
विश्वं पश्चात् पश्यन् इदन्तया निखिलमीश्वरो जात:। —षट्त्रिंशत्संदोह 4
राजानकानन्द explains एवं क्रमावभासनात् विश्वस्य ---अत्र
वेद्यजातस्य स्फुटावभासनात् ज्ञानशक्त्युद्रेक:। आन्तरदशाया
उद्रिक्तत्वात् सदाशिवावस्था बहिर्भावपरतोद्रेकात्तु
ईश्वरावस्था इत्यनयोर्विशेष:।
36. ईश्वरो बहिरुन्मेषो निमेषोन्त: सदाशिव:। —महार्थमञ्जरी p. 42
37. मध्यमे तु रूपे 'अहमिदम्' इति समधृततुलापुटेन यो विमर्श:। —प्रह. 3
38. अहन्तेदन्तयोरैक्यप्रतिपत्ति: शुद्धविद्या। —पराप्रावेशिका p. 7
39. सामानाधिकरण्यश्च, सद्विद्याऽहमिदं धियो:। —ईप्र. III. 1. 3
40. माया विभेदबुध्दिर्निजांशजातेषु सकलजीवेषु।
Commentator
—षट्त्रिंशत्सन्दोह कारिका 8
राजानक explains तत्र-तत्र भिन्न-भिन्न-प्रथात्मक-मायीय-
मलेन स्वांगकल्पेषु अपि जडवेद्यवर्गेषु विभिन्नतया बुद्धिरेव
मायाख्यं तत्त्वम्। This view is endorsed by Abhinavagupta in
तंत्रसार pp. 77-78
41.A स्व-स्वरूपेषु भावेषु भेदप्रथा माया। Abhinava says
अवभासकारिणी च परमेश्वरस्य मायानाम शक्ति:। —तंत्रसार pp. 77-79
41.B तत् सर्वकर्तृताशक्ति: संकुचिता कतिपयार्थमात्रपरा।
किञ्चित्कर्तारमभुं कलयन्ती कीर्त्यते कला नाम॥
42-43. सर्वज्ञतास्य शक्ति परिमितितनुरस्यवेद्यमात्रपरा।
ज्ञानमुत्पादयन्ती विद्यते निगद्यते बुद्धिराद्यै:॥ 9
44. नित्यपरिपूर्णतृप्ति: शक्तिस्तस्यैव परिमिता तु सती।
भोगेषु रञ्जयन्ती सततमभुं रागतत्त्वतां यात:॥ 10
45. सा नित्यताऽस्य शक्तिर्निष्कृष्य निधनोदयप्रदानेन।
नियत: परिच्छेदकरी क्लृप्ता स्यान् कालतत्त्वरूपेण।।
46. याऽस्य स्वतन्त्रताख्या शक्ति: संकोचशालिनी चैव।
कृत्याकृत्येष्ववशं नियतमभुं नियमन्त्यभून्नियति:।। —षट्त्रिंशत्संदोह: pp. 6-8

47. पूर्णत्वाभावेन परिमितत्त्वाद् अणुत्त्वम्। —प्रह.
48. गुणानामविभागावस्था प्रकृतित्त्वम्। —राजानक on षट्त्रिंशत्-संदोह-कारिका 13
49. एतत् त्रयमन्तःकरणम्। —पराप्रावेशिका p. 10
50. बुद्धिरध्यवसायस्य कारणं निश्चितात्मनः। —अनुत्तर-प्रकाश-पंचाशिका Kārikā 27
also तत्र बुद्धिरध्यवसायसामान्यरूपी। अभिनव on ई. प्र. वि. pp. 21-22
51. निश्चयकारिणी विकल्पप्रतिबिम्बधारणी बुद्धिः। क्षेम, पराप्रवेशिका p. 10
52. ज्ञानादिसत्वरूपा निर्णयबोधस्य कारणं बुद्धि। —षट्त्रिंशत्-संदोह-कारिका 15
On this Rajanaka remarks सत्त्वपरिणामिनी
ज्ञानशक्तिरेव अर्थाध्यवसायलक्षणा बुद्धिः।
53. अहंकारो नाम ममेदं नममेदं इत्यभिमानसाधनम्। —पराप्रावेशिका p. 10
54. अज्ञानं किल बन्धहेतुरुदितः शास्त्रे मलं तत् स्मृतम्। —तंत्रसार p. 5
55. स्वयं बध्नाति देवेशः स्वयमेव विमुञ्चति। तंत्रालोक 8- 82
56. ईश्वरेच्छावशादस्य भोगेच्छा संप्रजायते।
भोगसाधनसंसिध्यै भोगेच्छोरस्य मन्त्रराट्।
जगदुत्पादयामास मायामाविश्य शक्तिभिः। —तंत्रालोकटीका 6.56
57. शरीरभुवनाकारो मायीयः परिकीर्तितः। —तंत्रालोक 1-56
58. आवेशश्चास्वतंत्रस्य स्वतद्रूपनिमज्जनात्।
यस्तद्रूपता शम्भोः आद्याच्छवन्त्यविभागिनः।। —तंत्रालोक 1.205
59. हतं (हउं) सिवणाहु निहिल—जअतन्तसुनिब्भरोत्ति विरूरी।
फुरइविमरिस-भमरि पपलाअ (=प्रकाश) णिअलच्छी बिभइरी।। —तंत्रसार p. 34
SK. Chāyā of the above:
60. सर्वो ममायं विभवः इत्येवं परिजानतः।
विश्वात्मानो विकल्पानां प्रसरेऽपि महेशत्ता।। —ई प्र IV-1.12
SK. Chāyā of 59
अहं शिवनाथो निखिलजगत्तत्व सुनिर्भर इति विरावं
कुर्वन् (=कृत्वा)। स्फुरति विमर्श-भ्रमरः प्रकाश-निजलक्ष्य बिभर्ति।।
61. विकल्प हानेनैकाग्र्यात् क्रमेणेश्वरतापदम्। —ईप्रवि IV. 1-11
62. अन्तर्लक्ष्यो बहिर्दृष्टिः निमिषोन्मेषवर्जितः।
एषा वै शाम्भवी मुद्रा सर्वशास्त्रेषु गोपिता।।
63. स्वयंप्रकाशं शिवमाविशेत् क्षणात्।
64. दीयते ज्ञानसद्भावः क्षीयने पशुबन्धना।
दान-क्षपण-संयुक्ता दीक्षा तेनेह कीर्तिता।। —तंत्रालोक I. 80
65. दीक्षया मुच्यते जन्तुः प्रातिभेन तथा प्रिये।
गुर्वायत्ता तु सा दीक्षा बध्य-बन्धन-मोक्षणे।
प्रातिभोऽस्य स्वभावस्तु केवलीभावसिध्दिदः।। —तंत्रालोक VIII. 70
66. इत्थं श्रीशक्तिपातोऽयं निरपेक्ष इहोदितः। —तंत्रालोक VIII. 73
67. नायमात्मा प्रवचनेन लभ्यो, न मेधया, न बहुना श्रुतेन।
यमैवेष वृणुते तेन लभ्यः तस्यैव आत्मा विवृणुते तनूं स्वाम्।।
—कठ II. 23, मुण्डक III. 2;3.
68. आवेशश्चास्वतन्त्रस्य स्वतद्रूपनिमज्जनात्, परतद्रूपता शम्भोः। —तंत्रालोक I. 205
69. वस्तुस्थित्यां न बन्धोऽस्ति, तदाभावान्न मुक्तता।

70. बन्धमोक्षौ न भिद्येते सर्वत्रैव शिवत्वतः। —शिवदृष्टि 3.6
Utpala explains: अज्ञानलक्षणा सा च संसारो बन्ध उच्यते।
इति स्थितौ अज्ञानरूपौ बन्धमोक्षौ।
71. Utpala on शिवदृष्टि 3.70: शिवाभेदप्रतीतिमात्रं मोक्षः। तदप्रतीतिस्तु बन्धः।
72. मोक्षो हि नाम नैवान्यत् स्वरूपप्रथमं हि तत्।
स्वरूपं आत्मनः संवित्...। —तंत्रालोक I. 156
73. जगता निजानंदात्मना विश्वेन रूपेणानन्दः यत्र
यतश्चेति जगदानन्दशब्दवाच्यम्। —जयरथ on तंत्रालोक V. 50
74. स्वातन्त्र्यं नाम यथेच्छं तत्रेच्छाप्रसरस्य अविघातः। —ईप्रवि [.5.13]
75. चितिः प्रत्यवमर्शात्मा परावाक् स्वरसोदिता।
स्वातन्त्र्यमेतन्मुख्यं तदैश्वर्यं परात्मनः।
सास्फुरत्ता, महासत्ता, देशकाल विशेषिणी।
सैषा सारतया प्रोक्ता हृदयं परमेष्ठिनः।। —ई प्र. I. 5. 13-14
76. तस्माद् अपह्नवनीयः प्रकाश-विमर्शात्मा संवित्स्वभावः
परमशिवो भगवान् स्वातन्त्र्यादेव रूद्रादित्य स्थावरान्त-प्रमातृरूपतया, नील-सुखादिप्रमेय-
रूपतया य अनरिक्तयाऽपि अतिरिक्तया
इव स्वरूपानाच्छादिकया संविविद्रूपनानन्तरीयिकस्वातन्त्र्य-
महिम्ना प्रकाशत इति अयं स्वातन्त्र्यवाद : प्रोन्मीलितः। —ईप्रवि Introduction
77. दर्पणबिम्बे यद्वनं नगरग्रामादि चित्रमविभागि।
भाति विभागेनैव च परस्परं दर्पणादपि च।
विमलतम-परमभैरव-बोधात् तद्वत् विभागशून्यमपि।
अन्योन्यं च ततोऽपि च विभक्तमाभाति जगदेतम्॥ 13 —परमार्थसारकारिका 12-13
78. चिदात्मैव हि देवोऽन्तः स्थितिमिच्छावशाद् बहिः।
योगीव निरुपादानमर्थजातं प्रकाशयेत्।। —ईप्र. I. 5-7

Chapter 3

1. सुघट एष मार्गो नवो। —ई. प्र. IV. I. 16
2. निराभासात् पूर्णादहमिति पुरा भासयति यद्।
द्विशाखामाशास्ते तदनु च विभङ्क्तुं निजकलाम्।।
स्वरूपादुन्मेष-प्रसरणनिमेष-स्थिति जुषस्।
तदद्वैतं वन्दे परमशिवशक्त्यात्मनिखिलम्।।—ई प्र. 2.9
निराभासात्=शिवशक्त्यादिरूपेभ्यः आभासेभ्यो
निष्क्रान्तात् एकत्वेन शिवशक्त्यादि विकल्परहितात्। —भास्करकण्ठ
3. सर्वभाष्यमतौ यद्वा कुत्रापि सुमहाधियि।
न वाऽन्यन्नापि तु स्वात्मन्येषा स्थादुयकारिणी।। —ईप्र. Intro. V. 6
स्वात्मनि=स्वात्मतुस्येषु पुत्रादिषु शिष्येषु च —भास्कर
4. कथंचिदासाद्य महेश्वरस्य
दास्यं जनस्याप्युपकारमिच्छन्।

समस्तसम्पत्समवाप्तिहेतुम्
तत्प्रत्यभिज्ञामुपपादयामि।। —ईप्र. V.I, p. 18

5. यद्यपि आयातदृढेश्वरशक्तिपालस्य स्वयमेवेयमियती परमशिवममिरभ्येति हृदयगोचरं, न तु अत्र स्वात्मीयः पुरुषकारः कोऽपि निर्वहति। op. cit., pp. 20-21
6. तस्मात् सुत्रार्थं मन्दबुद्धीन् प्रतीत्थम्। [प्रति+इत्थम्] सम्यग् व्याख्यास्ये प्रत्यभिज्ञा-विविक्त्यै।।5।। —IPV p. 15
7. दीयते अस्मै स्वामिना सर्वं यथाभिलषितप् इति दासः। —IPV p. 29
8. यमधिकृत्य पुरुषः प्रवर्तते तत् प्रयोजनम्।
9. It is a clever use of उप and अप with √याच् in
   भक्तिलक्ष्मीसमृद्धानां किमन्यद् उप-याचितम्।
   एतया च दरिद्राणां किमन्यद् अप-याचितम्।
10. Dr. Pandey's translation of the verse समस्तसम्पत्-समवाप्ति
11. Dr. Pandey's translation of the verse
    प्रकाशस्यात्मविश्रान्तिरहंभावो हि कीर्तितः।
    उक्ताच सैव विश्रान्तिः सर्वापेक्षानिरोधतः।
    स्वातन्त्र्यमकर्तृत्वं मुख्यमीश्वरतापि वा। —IPV I. p. 35
12. भात-भासमान-रूपानुसन्धानान्मिका। —IPV. I. p. 36
    Abhinava defines प्रत्यभिज्ञा as follows:
    प्रत्यभिज्ञा च - भात-भासमानरूपानुसन्धानात्मिका,
    स एवायं च चैत्रः (name of a person) इति प्रतिसंधानेन अभिमुखीभूते वस्तुनि ज्ञानम्...अन्ततोऽपि सामान्यात्मना
    वा ज्ञातस्य पुनरभिमुखीभावावसरे प्रतिसंधिप्राणितमेव ज्ञानं प्रत्यभिज्ञा।
    —IPV pp. 36.37

13.A Prose order of the verse quote in note 4:
महेश्वरस्य दास्यं समस्तसंपल्लाभहेतुं कथंचिदासाद्य,
जनस्यापि कथंचित् तत्प्रत्यभिज्ञाम् आसाद्य, प्रापथ्य,
उपकारं समस्तसंपलाभहेतुभूतं महेश्वरदास्यात्मकं इच्छान्
तामेव समस्तसंपत्समवायहेतुकां तत्प्रत्यभिज्ञाम् उपपादयामि—अभिनव IPV. p. 44

13. अनन्त-भाव-संभार-भासने स्पन्दनं परम्।
    उपोद्धातायमे यस्य तं स्तुमः सर्वदा शिवम्॥ —IPV. p. 47
14. स्वप्रकाशेऽपि वा ईश्वरे प्रमातृणां किंवृत्तं येन तेषां प्रमाणव्यापारानुपयोग, इत्याशङ्क्यऽऽह — op. cit., p. 47
    * कर्तरि ज्ञातरि स्वात्मन्यादिसिद्धे महेश्वरे।
    अजडात्मा निषेधं वा सिद्धिं वा विदधीत कः। —IP. I. 1
    ** न खलु सर्व-शव्दार्थो ज्ञातृ-कर्तृत्वयोः स्वरूपं भिनत्ति। —IPV p. 50
15. न हि प्रयत्नशतैरपि अग्निरनग्नितां नेतुं शक्यते। —भास्करकण्ठ op. cit., p. 51
16. तस्मात् विषयाभिमतं वस्तु शरीरतया गृहीत्वा
    तावत् निर्भासमान आत्मैव प्रकाशते विच्छेदशून्यः।
    सुषुप्तमपि प्रति प्रकाशत एव, अन्यथा स्मृत्ययोगतः

प्रकाशस्य च नित्यत्वात् विच्छेदहेतोरभावेन, अन्यप्रमात्र-
पेक्षया च प्रकाशमानत्वात्, स्वपरप्रमातृविभागस्य तत्सृष्टस्य
मायीयत्वेन वक्ष्यमाणत्वात्। —IPV. I. pp. 52-53

16.A ज्ञानपल्लवस्वभावा एव हि क्रिया। op. cit., p. 54

17. एतदेव माहेश्वर्यं यद् अनवच्छिन्नप्रकाशकत्वेन
ज्ञातृत्व-कर्तृत्वधारोपारोहः। op. cit., p. 55

18. न च जडात्मा स्वात्मन्यपि दुर्लभप्रकाशस्वातंत्र्य-लेशः
किञ्चित् साधयितुं निषेद्धुं वा प्रभविष्णुः पाषाण इव। op. cit., p. 55

19. It is a clever argument. If the Self as conceived *by Ajadātma-vādin* (one who believes that the Self is sentient) appears as new, it would mean that it did not shine before and was insentient. If the soul does not it is insentient and cannot prove or disprove Maheśvara. Therefore the light of the external object is non-different from the light of the self. The self is nothing but light. He is eternal and self-luminous. —op. cit., pp. 55-58

20. किन्तु मोहवशादस्मिन् दृष्टेऽप्यनुपलक्षिते।
शक्त्याविष्करणेनेयं प्रत्यभिज्ञोपदृश्यते।। IP.I. 2nd Kārikā

20.A यश्चायं मोहस्तदपसारणं च यत्, तदुभयमपि भगवत
एव विजृम्भामात्रम्, न तु अधिकं किञ्चित्। op. cit., p. 59

21. तथा हि जडभूतानां प्रतिष्ठा जीवदाश्रया।
ज्ञानं क्रिया च भूतानां जीवतां जीवनं मतम्।। IPI. 4th Kārikā

22. तेन यद् यया यावत् अबाधितं विमृश्यते तत् तावत्
तथा अस्ति। IPV. I p. 62

23. क्रिया-सम्बन्ध-सामान्य-द्रव्य-दिक्कालबुध्दयः।
सत्याः स्थैर्योपयोगाभ्यामेकानेकाश्रया मताः॥ —IP. II. 2-1

24. जीवा हि जडभेदात् भेदभागिनः, जडाश्च जीवभेदात्....
नील-पीतादिभावभेदास्तु प्रमातृसंलग्नतया भेदभूमिमेव
परमधिरूढा इति....तदेव जीवानामभेदः एव संपन्न इति
जीवन् प्रमाता-इतिजातम्। जीवनं च जीवकर्तृत्वं तच्च
ज्ञानक्रियात्मकम्, यो हि जानाति च करोति च स जीवति-इत्युच्यते।
तदयं प्रमाता ज्ञानक्रियाशक्तियोगाद् ईश्वर इति व्यवहर्तव्यः। op. cit., pp. 66-68

25. यो यावति ज्ञाता कर्ताच स तावति ईश्वरो राजेव,
अनीश्वरस्य ज्ञातृत्व-कर्तृत्वे स्वभाव-विरुद्धे यतः
आत्मा च विश्वत्र ज्ञाता कर्ता च - इति सिद्धा प्रत्यभिज्ञा। op. cit., p. 68

26. तत्र ज्ञानं स्वतः सिद्धं, क्रिया कायाश्रिता सती।
परैरप्युपलक्ष्येत तयान्यज्ञानमूह्यते॥ Ip. I. 1-5

27. तेन आन्तरी क्रियाशक्तिः ज्ञानवदेव स्वतः सिद्धा स्व-
प्रकाशा...सा च परशरीरादि-साहित्येन अवगता स्वं स्वभावं
ज्ञानात्मकं अवगमयति...इति परज्ञानं स्वात्मैव, परत्वं केवलं
उपाधेर्देहादेः...स चापि विचारितो यावत् न अन्यः इति
विश्वः प्रमातृवर्गः परमार्थतः एकः प्रमाता स च एव अस्ति। IPV pp. 74-76

28. घटो मदात्मना वेत्ति वेद्म्यहं च घटात्मना।
सदाशिवात्मना वेद्म्यहं (वेद्मि+अहं), स वा वेत्ति मदात्मना॥
नानाभावैः स्वमात्मानं जानन्नास्ते सदाशिवः। —सोमानंद-शिवदृष्टि
29. ततोऽयम् उपोद्घातः। <u>उप</u> इति आत्मनः समीपे टङ्कवत्
ईश्वरप्रज्ञाभिलक्षणः उत्कर्षः, <u>हन्यते</u> विश्राम्यते येन। एतावदेव
च अस्य ग्रंथस्य तात्पर्यम्। —IPV. pp. 78-79
30. अयम् उपोद्घातः। उपांशु अविततं कृत्वा, उद्इति शास्त्रस्य ऊर्ध्व एव हन्यते
अपासार्यत्ते प्रमेयविषयो व्यामोहः येन। —IPV. p. 79
31. अनन्तमानमेयादिवैचित्र्याभेदशालिनम्।
आत्मानं यः प्रथयते भक्तानां तं स्तुमः शिवम्॥ —ई. प्र. वि II. 209
32. स्वात्मैव सर्वजन्तूनामेक एव महेश्वरः।
विश्वरूपोऽहामिदमित्यखण्डामर्शबृंहितः॥ —ई. प्र. IV. 1-1
33. ई. प्रवि II p. 282
34. तत्र स्वसृष्टेदंभागे बुद्ध्यादिग्राहकात्मना।
अहंकारपरामर्शपदं नीतमनेन तत्॥ —ई. प्र. IV. 1-2
35. स स्वरूपापरिज्ञानमयोऽनेकः पुमान् मतः।
तत्र सृष्टौ क्रियानन्दौ भोगो दुःखसुखात्मकः॥ —ई. प्र. IV. 1-3
36. स्वाङ्गरूपेषु भावेषु पत्युर्ज्ञानं क्रिया च या।
मायातृतीये ते एव पशोः सत्वं रजस्तमः॥ —ई. प्र. IV. 1-4
37. भेदस्थितेः शक्तिमतः शक्तित्वं नापदिश्यते।
एषां गुणानां करण-कार्यत्व-परिणामिनाम्॥ —ई. प्र. IV. 1-5
38. सत्तानन्दाः क्रिया पत्युस्तदभावोऽपि सा पशोः।
द्व्यात्मा तद्रजो दुःखं श्लेषि सत्त्वतमोमयम्॥ —ई. प्र. IV. 1-6
39. भवनकर्तृता-'भू' क्रियाकर्तृत्वम्, अस्तीति सत्, तस्य
भावः सत्ता इति न्यायात् इति भावः। —भास्करकंठ, ई. प्र. वि. p. 289
40. अपि शब्दः चार्थे, पशोः सा सत्ता सत्त्वम्, तदभावः
नमः, द्व्यात्मा रजः —ई. प्र. वि. p. 291
41. येऽप्यसामयिकेदन्ता परामशभिुवः प्रभोः।
ते विमिश्रा विभिन्नाश्च तथा चित्रावभासिनः॥ —ई प्र. IV. 1-7
42. K.C. Pandey— IPV. III. p. 224
43. ते तु भिन्नावभासार्थाः प्रकल्प्याः(ल्-प्-या) प्रत्यगात्मनः।
तत्तद्विविभिन्नसंज्ञाभिः स्मृत्युत्प्रेक्षादिगोचरे॥ IP. IV. 1-8
44. ईश्वरस्य . . . शुद्धविमर्शविषयीभाव्या अर्थाः। IPV. II p. 295
45. तस्यासाधारणी सृष्टिरीशसृष्ट्युपजीवनी।
सैषाप्यज्ञतया सत्यैवेशशक्त्या तदात्मनः॥ 9॥
स्वविश्रान्त्युपरोधायाचलया प्राणरूपया।
विकल्पक्रियया तत्तद्वर्णवैचित्र्यरूपया॥ 10॥ IP. IV. 9-10
46. साधारणोऽन्यथा चैशः सर्गः स्पष्टावभासनात्।
विकल्पहानेनैकाग्र्त् क्रमेणेश्वरतापदम्॥ IP. IV. 1-11

47. अन्तर्लक्ष्यो बहिर्दृष्टिः निमिषोन्मेषवर्जितः।
एषा वै शाम्भवी मुद्रा, सर्वशास्त्रेषु गोपिता॥

48. परिज्ञातया ईशशक्त्या परिज्ञाततादात्म्यस्य भवति तदा सोऽपि साधारण एवं आप्यायनाभिचरणशान्त्यादिविकल्प इव न्यस्त-मन्त्रस्य भावितान्तःकरणस्य। IPV. II. p. 302

49. सर्वो ममायं विभवः इत्येवं परिजानतः।
विश्वात्मनो विकल्पानां प्रसरेऽपि महेशता॥ IP. IV. 1-12

50. मेयं साधारणं मुक्तः स्वात्माभेदेन मन्यते।
महेश्वरो यथा बद्धः पुनरत्यंतभेदवत्॥ IP. IV. 1-13

51. सर्वथा त्वन्तरालीनानन्ततत्त्वौघनिर्भरः।
शिवः चिदानन्द-घनः परमाक्षरविग्रहः॥ IP. IV. 1-14

52. एवमात्मानमेतस्य सम्यक् ज्ञान-क्रिये तथा।
जानन्यथेप्सितान् पश्यन् जानाति च करोति च॥ IP. IV. 1-15

53. इति प्रकटितो मया सुघट एष मार्गो नवो
महागुरुभिरुच्यते स्म शिवदृष्टिशास्त्रे यथा।
तदत्र निदधत् पदं भुवन-कर्तृतामात्मनो
विभाव्य शिवतामयीमनिशमाविशन्सिद्ध्यति॥ IP. IV. 1-16

54. तैस्तैरप्युपयाचितैरुपनस्तन्व्याः स्थितोऽप्यन्तिके
कान्तो लोकसमान एवमपरिज्ञातो न रन्तुं यथा।
लोकस्यैष तथानवेक्षितगुणः स्वात्मापि विश्वेश्वरो
नैवालं निजवैभवाय तदियं तत्प्रत्यभिज्ञोदिता॥ IP. IV. 1-17

55. जनस्यायत्नसिद्ध्यर्थमुदयाकरसूनुना।
ईश्वरप्रत्यभिज्ञेयमुत्पलेनोपपादिता॥ IP. IV. 1-18

56. वाक्य-प्रमाण-पद-तत्त्व सदागमार्थाः
स्वात्मोपयोगमुपयान्त्यमुतः स्वशास्त्रात्।
भौमान् रसाञ्जलमयांश्च न सस्यपुष्टौ
मुक्त्वार्कमेकमिह योजयितुं क्षमोऽन्यः॥
आत्मानमनभिज्ञाय विवेक्तुं योऽन्यदिच्छति।
तेन भौतेन किं वाच्यम् प्रश्नेऽस्मिन् को भवानिति॥
इति श्रीमदाचार्योत्पलदेवविरचितायामीश्वरप्रत्यभिज्ञायां
श्रीमदाचार्याभिनवगुप्तविरचित-विमर्शिन्याख्यटीकोपेतायां
तत्वसंग्रहमहाधिकारः। समाप्ता श्रीमदीश्वरप्रत्यभिज्ञा॥

Chapter 4

1. इह ये सुकुमारमतयोऽकृततीक्ष्णतर्कशास्त्रपरिश्रमाः। शक्तिपातोन्मिषित-पारमेश्वरसमावेशाभिलाषिणः कतिचित् भक्तिभाजः तेषाम् ईश्वरप्रत्यभिज्ञोपदेश-तत्त्वं मनाक् उन्मील्यते।
—प्रत्यभिज्ञा-हृदय p. 46

2. तस्मात् सूत्रार्थं मन्दबुद्धीन् प्रतीत्थं
सम्यग् व्याख्यास्ये प्रत्यभिज्ञाविविक्तयै [क्+त्+यै]
—ईश्वर-प्रत्यभिज्ञा-विमर्शिनी
Intro. Verse 5
3. सर्वत्रास्य मतौ यद्वा कुत्रापि सुमहाधियि।
न वाऽन्यत्रापि तु स्वात्मन्येषा स्यादुपकारिणी॥ —ईप्रवि. V. 6
4. आत्मानमनभिज्ञाय विवेक्तुं योऽन्यदिच्छति।
तेन भौतेन किं वाच्यं प्रश्नेऽस्मिन् को भवानिति॥ —ईप्रवि. II, p. 317
5. शांकरोपनिषत्-सार-प्रत्यभिज्ञामहोदधेः।
क्षेमेणोद्ध्रियते सारः संसारविषशान्तये॥ —प्र. ह. मंगल V. 2
6. तत्र स्वात्मदेवताया एव सर्वत्र कारणत्वं सुखोपाय-
प्राप्यत्वं महाफलत्त्वं च अभिव्यङ्तुम् आह। —प्र. ह. p. 46
7. अस्थास्यदेकरूपेण वपुषा चेन्महेश्वरः।
महेश्वरत्वं संवित्त्वं तदत्यक्षद् घटादिवत्॥ —तंत्रालोक 3-900
8. प्रकाशरूपा चिच्छक्तिः। —तंत्रसार I. P. 6
स च प्रकाशो न परतन्त्रः . . न च प्रकाशान्तरं किञ्चिद्
अस्ति इति स्वतन्त्रः। —Ibid
9. विमर्शो नाम विश्वाकारेण, विश्वप्रकाशनेन, विश्वसंहरणेन,
अकृत्रिमाहमिति विस्फुरणम्। —पराप्रावेशिका pp. 1-2
10. यदि निर्विमर्शः स्यात् अनीश्वरो जडश्च प्रसज्येत। —Ibid
11. चितिः स्वतन्त्रा विश्वसिद्धिहेतुः। —प्र. हृ. सू.,
12. सर्वाःशक्तीः कर्तृत्वशक्तिः ऐश्वर्यात्मा समाक्षिपति
सा च विमर्शरूपा। —ईप्रवि I 5.15 on Page 267
13. स्पन्दनं च किञ्चिच्चलनं, एषैव किञ्चिद्रूपता यत्
अचलमपि चलमाभासते। —ईप्रवि I. 256-57
14. सत्ता च भवनकर्तृता सर्वक्रियासु स्वातन्त्र्यम्।
—ईप्रवि. 238-59
also सा स्फुरत्ता, महासत्ता etc in ईप्र. I. 514
15. इति व्यापक-नित्योदित-परिपूर्णरूपा इयम् इत्यर्थ-
लभ्यमेव एतत्। —प्र.हृ. (सू) (page) 47
16. स्वेच्छया स्वभित्तौ विश्वमुन्मीलयति। —प्र.हृ. 2
17. जगतः प्रकाशैकात्म्येन अवस्थानम् उक्त। —प्र.हृ. 2-52
18. तन्नाना अनुरूप ग्राह्यग्राहकभेदात्। —प्र.हृ. 3
19. Vide Supra the evolution of the universe (विश्व). Śiva manifests himself in all the 36 Tattvas
20. मायोर्ध्वे शुद्धविद्याधः सन्ति विज्ञानकेवलाः। —प्र.हृ. 3-53
21. श्रमित्परमशिवस्य . . . एवंविधमेव . . . अखिलमभेदेनैव
स्फुरति; न तु वस्तुतः अन्यत् किञ्चित् ग्राह्यं वा ग्राहकं वा,
अपि तु श्रीपरमशिवभट्टारक एवं इत्थं नानावैचित्र्यसहस्रैः स्फुरति। —प्र.हृ. 3-54
22. चितिसंकोचात्मा चेतनोऽपि संकुचित-विश्वमयः। —प्र.हृ. 4

23. In this state, Śiva is called '*Anāśrita Śiva*'. As Śiva is not related to anything or has no objective content, this state is intermediate between *Śakti Tattva* and *Sadāśiva Tattva,* In this state Śakti begins to isolate the universe from the self by producing ignorance (*akhyāti*) about his nature. The self forgets its identity (*I-ness*) with the universe. This loss of experience is *Saṁsāra.*
24. The verse quoted by Kṣema is a combination of verses 3-A and 4-A of the second Niṣyanda of the *Spanda Kārikā*
25. एतत् तत्त्व परिज्ञानमेव मुक्तिः एतत्तत्त्वापरिज्ञानमेव बन्धः। —प्र.हृ. 4-58
26. चितिरेव चेतनपदादवरूढा चेत्यसंकोचिनी चित्तम्। —प्र.हृ. 5
27. न चित्तं नाम अन्यत् किञ्चित्, अपितु सैव भगवती (चिति) तत्। —प्र.हृ. 5-59
28. The verse is:
स्वाङ्गरूपेषु भावेषु पत्युर्ज्ञानं क्रिया च या।
माया तृतीये ते एव पशोः सत्यं रजस्तमः॥ —ई.प्र.वि. IV 1-4
29. तन्मयो (चित्तमयः) माया प्रमाता। —प्र.हृ. 6
30. चित्तमात्मा। —शिवसूत्र III 7
31. स चैको द्विरूपः त्रिमयः। चतुरात्मा सप्तपञ्चकस्वभावः। —प्र.हृ. 7
32. प्रकाशरूपत्त्व-संकोचावभासवत्त्वाभ्यां 'द्विरूपः' —प्र.हृ. 7.63
33. तद्भूमिका : सर्वदर्शनस्थितयः। —प्र.हृ. 8
34. Kṣema interprets *asat* (असत्) in the Upaniṣadic sentences असदेव सोम्य--इदम् अग्र आसीत् as शून्य and equates that statement with शून्यवाद. But *asat* in that sentence means 'un-manifest'. It means "What was unmanifest became manifest".
35. अत एक एव एतावद् व्याप्तिक आत्मा। —प्र.हृ. 8-68
36. This *Vidyā kañcuka* does not allow the jīvātman (जीवात्मन्) to take a holistic view of 'quality'
37. एषा च भट्टारिका क्रमात्क्रमं अधिकमनुशील्यमाना स्वात्मसात् करोति एव भक्तजनम्। —प्र.हृ. 8-71
38. चिद्वत्-तच्छक्तिसंकोचात् मलावृतः संसारी। —प्र.हृ. 9
39. तथाविधश्च अयं शक्तिदरिद्रः संसारी उच्यते स्वशक्ति-विकासे तु शिव एव। —प्र.हृ. 9-73
40. तथापि तद्वत् पञ्चकृत्यानि करोति। —प्र.हृ. 10
41. सृष्टिसंहारकर्तारं विलयस्थितिकारकम्।
अनुग्रहकरं देवं प्रणतार्तिविनाशनम्॥ —स्वच्छन्दतंत्र I. 3
42. अत एव ये सदा एतत् [पञ्चविधकृत्यकारित्वम्] परि-शीलयन्ति, ते स्वरूपविकासमयं विश्वं जानाना जीवन्मुक्ता इति आम्नाताः। ये तु न तथा ते...बद्धात्मानः। —प्र.हृ. 10. 75-76
43. आभासन-शक्ति-विमर्शन-बीजावस्थापन-विलपनतस्तानि। —प्र.हृ.-II
44. ईदृशं पञ्चविधकृत्यकारित्वं . . . सद्गुरूपदेशं विना न प्रकाशते, तस्मात् सद्गुरुसपर्या एव एतत् प्रथार्थं अनुसर्तव्था। —प्र.हृ. II-78
45. तदपरिज्ञाने स्वशक्तिभिर्व्यामोहितता संसारित्वम्। —प्र.हृ. 12

46. मन्त्रा वर्णात्मकाः सर्वे, सर्वे वर्णाः शिवात्मकाः।
quoted by Kṣema from सर्व-वीरभट्टारक
47. In this Mudrā, the eyes are open without
winking of the eyelids but the attention is within (toward the Self)
अन्तर्लक्ष्यो बहिर्दृष्टिः निमिषोन्मेषवर्जितः।
इयं सा भैरवी मुद्रा, सर्वतन्त्रेषु गोपिता॥
48. सर्वो ममायं विभव इत्येवं परिजानतः।
विश्वात्मानो विकल्पानां प्रसरेऽपि महेशता॥ —ईप्र. IV. 11-12
49. इत्येवं निजशक्तिव्यामोहितता एव संसारित्वम्। —प्र.हृ. I. 2-83
50. निःश्वासोच्छ्वासकासाश्च प्राणकर्मेतिकीर्तिताः।
अपानवायोः कर्मैतत् विण्मूत्रादि-विसर्जनम्॥
उदानकर्म तत्प्रोक्तं देहस्योन्नयनादि यत्।
पोषणादि समानस्य शरीरे कर्म कीर्तितम्॥ —योगी याज्ञवल्क्य IV. 66-68
51. Compare the positions of these vital airs (Prāṇas) given as follows in *Gorakṣa Saṁhitā*.
हृदि प्राणो वसेन्नित्यम्, अपानो गुह्यमंडले।
समानो नाभिदेशे तु, उदानः कण्ठमध्यगः।
व्यानो व्यापी शरीरे तु प्रधानाः पञ्चधातवः॥ —गोरक्षसंहिता 30
52. Based on note no. 120 (in Jaideva Singh's edition of *Prty. Hṛdaya*) p. 144
53. मनुष्यदेहमास्थाय छन्नास्ते परमेश्वराः। —Āgama quoted in *Prtyabhijñā-Hṛdaya* p. 85
54. शरीरमेव घटाद्यपि ये षट्त्रिंशत्तत्वमयं शिवरूपतया पश्यन्ति
तेऽपि सिध्यन्ति। Quoted in प्र.हृ. 12 from ईप्रवि
55. तत्परिज्ञाने चित्तमेव अन्तर्मुखीभावेन चेतनपदाध्यारोहात् चितिः। —प्र.हृ. 13
56. चितिवह्निः अवरोहपदे छिन्नोऽपि मात्रया मेयेन्धनं प्लुष्यति। —प्र.हृ. 14
57. वर्त्तन्ते जन्तवोऽशेषा अपि ब्रह्मेन्द्रविष्णवः।
ग्रसमानास्ततो वन्दे देव विश्वं भवन्मयम्॥
—प्र.हृ. Quotation from—उत्पल, शिवस्तोत्रावली XX. 17
58. बललाभे विश्वमात्मसात् करोति। —प्र.हृ. 15
59. यथा वह्निः उद्बोधितो दाह्यं दहति, तथा विषयपाशान् भक्षयेत्। —प्र.हृ. 15.90
60. एषा (चितिः) तु सदैव प्रकाशमानाः अन्यथा तत् देहादि
अपि न प्रकाशेत। —प्र.हृ. 15.90
61. अत एव देहादि-प्रमातृताभिमान निमज्जनाय अभ्यासः, न तु
सदा प्रथमानतासार प्रमातृता-प्राप्त्यर्थम्। —प्रत्यभिज्ञा Quoted in प्र.हृ. 15.91
62. चिदानन्दलाभे देहादिषु चेत्यमानेष्वपि
चिदैकात्म्यप्रतिपत्तिदार्ढ्यं जीवन्मुक्तिः। —प्र.हृ. 16
63. इति वा यस्य संवित्तिः क्रीडात्वेनाखिलं जगत्।
स पश्यन् सततं मुक्तो जीवन्मुक्तो न संशयः॥ —स्पन्दकारिका II. 5
64. मध्यविकासात् चिदानन्दलाभः। —प्र.हृ. 17
65. प्राक् संवित्प्राणे परिणता। —प्र.हृ. 17. 93
66. *Prāṇāyāma* is breath-control. *Mudrā*—certain positions of fingers (e.g. *Yonī Mudrā*) and of the tongue as in *Khecarī Mudrā*. The *Gheraṇḍa*

Saṁhitā gives ten *Mudrās*. *Bandha* is contracting certain organs of the body e.g. *Mūla Bandha, Uḍḍīyāna Bandha, Jālandhara Bandha, Mahā Bandhā*.

For details—*Pātañjala Yoga Pradīpa*. pp. 433-446

67. विकल्पहानेन ऐकाग्र्यात् क्रमेणेश्वरता-पदम्। —ईप्र. IV. 9 11B

68. यदा क्षोभ: प्रलीयेत तदा स्यात् परमं पदम्। —स्पन्दकारिका I. 9

69. शक्तेर्विकास: अन्तर्गूढाया अक्रममेव सकल-करण-चक्र-विस्फारणेन। —प्र.हृ. 18-98

70. अन्तर्लक्ष्यो बहिर्दृष्टि: निमिषोन्मेषवर्जित:। —प्र.हृ. 18-98

71. रूपादिषु परिणामात् तत्सिद्धि:। —प्र.हृ. 18-98

By transformation he means: This *siddhi* is accomplished by viewing the consciousness that considers itself outgoing as the same that is inward even in the presence of objects. (रूपादिषु)

72. पराञ्चि खानि व्यतृणत् स्वयंभू:
तस्मात् पराङ् पश्यति नान्तरात्मन्।
कश्चिद्धीर: प्रत्यगात्मानमैक्षद्
आवृत्तचक्षु: अमृतत्वमश्नन्॥ —कठोपनिषत् 4-1

73. सर्वा: शक्ती:चेतसा दर्शनाद्या:
स्वे स्वे वेद्ये यौगपद्येन विश्वक्।
क्षिप्त्वा मध्ये हाटकस्तम्भभूत:-
तिष्ठन् विश्वाधार एकोऽवभासि॥

74. वह्नेर्विषस्य मध्ये तु चित्तं सुखमयं क्षिपेत्।
केवलं वायुपूर्णं वा स्मरानन्देन युज्यते॥ —विज्ञानभैरव 66

75. अनच्ककृत्तायति प्रसृतपार्श्वनाडीद्वय-
च्छिदो विधृतचेतसो हृदयपङ्कजस्योदरे।
उदेति तव दारित्तान्धतमस: स विद्याङ्कुरो
य एष परमेशतां जनयितु पशोरप्यलम्॥

The last two lines of this verse state that thereby (practice mentioned above) darkness of ignorance is 'shattered'. The sprout of your knowledge capable of granting Śivahood to Paśus manifests (=arises)

76. यथा तथा यत्र यत्र द्वादशान्ते मन: क्षिपेत्।
प्रतिक्षणं क्षीणवृत्तेर्वैलक्षण्यं दिनैर्भवेत्॥ —विज्ञानभैरव 51

77. एकचिन्ताप्रसक्तस्य यत: स्यादपरोदय:।
उन्मेष: स तु विज्ञेय: स्वयं तदुपलक्षयेत्॥ —स्पन्दकारिका III. 9

78. जग्धि-पान-कृतोल्लास-रसानन्द-विजृम्भणात्।
भावयेत् भरितावस्थां महानंदमयो भवेत्॥ 726
गीतादिविषयास्वादासमसौख्यैकतात्मन:।
योगिनस्तन्मयत्वेन मनोरूढे स्तदात्मता॥ 734
यत्र यत्र मनस्तुष्टिर्मनस्तत्रैव धारयेत्।
तत्र तत्र परानन्दस्वरूपं संप्रकाशते॥ 744 —विज्ञानभैरव 72-74

79. समाधिसंस्कारवति व्युत्थाने भूयोभूय: चिदैक्यामर्शान्
नित्योदित समाधि:। —प्र.हृ. 19

80. In this Samādhi eyes are closed. With his closed eyes in inward *Samādhi,* his individual consciousness merges completely into the universal consciousness. This is real introversion (*antar-mukhatā*) with no trace of external object left.

81. क्रममुद्रया अन्तःस्वरूपया बहिर्मुखः समाविष्टो
भवति साधकः। —प्र.हृ. 19
अन्तः स्वरूपया-By the essential nature of the perfect "I".

82. तत्रादौ बाह्यात् अन्तःप्रवेशः, आभ्यन्तरात् बाह्यस्वरूपे
प्रवेशः आवेशवशात् जायते - इति सबाह्यान्तरोऽयं मुद्राक्रमः। —प्र.हृ. 19. 104

83. तदा प्रकाशानन्दसार-महामन्त्रवीर्यात्मक-पूर्णाहन्ता
आवेशात् सदा सर्व-सर्ग-संहारकारि-निजसंविद्देवता -
चक्रेश्वरता-प्राप्तिः भवति —इति शिवम्। —प्र.हृ. 20

84. From universal point of view, these *Saṁvid-devatās* are *Khecarī-cakra, Dikcarī-cakra* and *Bhūearī-cakra* mentioned previously. From individual point of view these are limited knowledge, internal and external sense-organs and limited objective knowledge.

85. *Kālāgni-bhuvaneśa Rudra* is the lowest stage of creation on manifestation while *Śāntā kalā* is the highest stage of manifestation.

86. Words are classified as *Māyīya* (pertaining to Māyā) and *a-Māyīya* (not pertaining to Māyā). Meanings are conventionally attributed to *Māyīya* words and they are *Vikalpas.* But *a-Māyīya* words are *nīrvikalpa,* the meaning of which is real that is not depending on conventions as in the case of *Vikalpa.*

87. *Jagadānanda* — The bliss of the self appearing as the universe. The universe is the bliss of the Lord made manifest

88. कुलं शक्तिरिति प्रोक्तं, अकुलं शिव उच्यते। —स्वच्छन्दतन्त्र

89. As in Pāṇinī's sūtras- अच् means all the vowels अ,आ, इ etc. Here *a* (अ) and- *ha* (ह) is to be combined

90. प्रकाशस्य आत्मविश्रान्तिरहंभावो हि कीर्तितः।
उक्ता च सैव विश्रान्तिः सर्वापेक्षानिरोधतः।
स्वातन्त्र्यमथकर्तृत्वं मुख्यमीश्वारतापि च॥ —अजड-प्रमातृ-सिद्धि 22-23

91. तदाक्रम्य बलं मन्त्राः सर्वत्र बलशालिनः।
प्रवर्तन्तेऽधिकाराय करणानीव देहिनाम्॥
तयैव संप्रलीयन्ते शान्तरूपा निरञ्जनाः।
सहाराधकचित्तेन तेन ते शिवधर्मिणः॥

Kṣema's interpretation:

On the basis of (resorting to) the power of *Spanda Tattva* (the deities of) Mantras become all-powerful and start functioning like the sense-organs of (human) beings. After performing their duties, they of pure *Saṁvid* in form, lose their deity form and get merged along with the mind of the aspirant in the *Spanda Tattva* or *Cidākāśa.* Hence these mantras are of the nature of Śiva

92. तद् अस्फुरणे कस्यापि अस्फुरणात्। —प्र.हृ. 20. P. III
93. मायाशक्त्या विभोः सैव भिन्नसंवेद्यगोचरा।
कथिता ज्ञानसंकल्प-अध्यवसायादि-नामभिः॥ —ईप्र. ज्ञानाधिकार. V. 18. I.P.I.18
94. सा चैषा प्रतिभा तत्तत् पदार्थक्रमरूषिता।
अक्रमानन्तचिद्रूपः प्रमाता स महेश्वरः॥ —ईप्र. ज्ञानाधिकार. VII. I.P.I.7.1
95. यदा त्वेकत्र संरूढस्तदा तस्य लयोद्भवौ।
नियच्छन् भोक्तृतामेति, ततश्चक्रेश्वरो भवेत्॥ —स्पंदकारिका III. 19
96. एकत्रारोपयेत् सर्वम्। —स्पंदकारिका III
97. Kṣema says that Kallaṭa's interpretation of *ekatra* 'in one place in gross or subtle body' should not he accepted. I *did* accept it in my Marathi edition of the *Spanda Karītā* as Kallaṭa was a direct disciple of Vasugupta and is expected to know what his teacher meant by *'ekatra'*. Kṣema belongs to the fourth generation after Vasugupta.
98. स्वतन्त्रः चितिचक्राणां चक्रवर्त्ती महेश्वरः।
संवित्ति-देवता-चक्र-जुष्टः कोऽपि जयत्यसौ॥
99. देह-प्राण-सुखादिभिः प्रतिकलं संरूध्यमानो जनः।
पूर्णानन्दघनामिमां न चिनुते माहेश्वरीं स्वां चितिम्॥
मध्ये बोधसुधाब्धिविश्वमभितः तत् फेनपिण्डोपमम्।
यः पश्येदुपदेशतस्तु कथितः साक्षात् स एकः शिवः॥
100. येषां वृत्तः शांकरः शक्तिपातो
येऽनभ्यासात् तीक्ष्णयुक्तिष्वयोग्याः।
शक्ता ज्ञातुं नेश्वरप्रत्यभिज्ञा-
मुक्तस्तेषामेष तत्त्वोपदेशः॥ - P.H. Last two verses

Chapter 5

1. सूत्रं वृत्तिर्विवृतिर्लघ्वी बृहत्युभे विमर्शिन्यौ।
प्रकरण-विवरण-पञ्चकमिति शास्त्रं प्रत्यभिज्ञायाः॥
2. कथंचिदासाद्य महेश्वरस्य
दास्यं जनस्याप्युपकारमिच्छन्।
समस्त-सम्पत्-समवाप्तिहेतुं
तत् प्रत्यभिज्ञामुपपादयामि॥ IP. 1. I
3. एकवारं प्रमाणेन शास्त्राद्वा गुरुवाक्यतः।
ज्ञाते शिवत्वे सर्वस्वे प्रतिपत्त्या दृढात्मनः॥
करणेन नास्ति कृत्यं क्वापि भावनयापि वा।
ज्ञाने सुवर्णे करणं भावनां वा परिष्यजेत्॥ —शिवदृष्टि
4. भक्तिलक्ष्मीसमृद्धानां किमन्यद् उपयाचितम्।
एतया वा दरिद्राणां किमन्यदपयाचितम्॥ —Quoted by Abhinava in IP. I. 1-1 p. 34

5. Abhinava remarks about प्रत्यभिज्ञा:
सामान्यात्मना वा ज्ञातस्य पुनरभिमुखी भावावसरे प्रतिसन्धि-
प्राणितमेव ज्ञानं प्रत्यभिज्ञा। IPV. I. p. 37
6. कर्तरि ज्ञातरि स्वात्मन्यादिसिद्धे महेश्वरे।
अजडात्मा-निषेधं वा सिद्धिं वा विदधीत क:॥ I.P. I. 1-2
7. किंतु मोहवशादस्मिन् दृष्टेऽप्यनुपलक्षिते।
शक्त्याविष्करणेनेयं प्रत्यभिज्ञोपदर्श्यते॥
तथा हि जडभूतानां प्रतिष्ठा जीवदाश्रया।
ज्ञानं क्रिया च भूतानां जीवितां जीवनं मतम्।
तत्र ज्ञानं स्वत: सिद्धं क्रिया कार्याश्रिता* सती
परैरप्युपलक्ष्येत तयान्यज्ञानमूह्यते॥ IP I. I. 3-5
8. सा चैषा प्रतिभा तत्तत्पदार्थक्रमरूषिता।
अक्रमानन्तचिद्रूप: प्रमाता स महेश्वर:॥ I. P. I. 7-1
9. तदैक्येन विना न स्यात् संविदां लोकपद्धति:।
प्रकाशैक्यात् तदेकत्वं मातैक: स इति स्थितम्॥
स एव विमृशत्वेन नियतेन महेश्वर:।
विमर्श एव देवस्य शुद्धे ज्ञान-क्रिये यथा॥ IP. I.8. 10-11
10. एष चानन्तशक्तित्वाद् एवमाभासयत्यमून्।
भावान् इच्छावशादेषा क्रिया निर्मातृताऽस्य सा॥ IP. II. 4-1
11. इत्थं तथा घट-पटाद्याभासजगदात्मना।
तिष्ठासोरेवमिच्छैव हेतुता, कर्तृता, क्रिया॥ IP. II. 4-21
Abhinava adds to explain the above verse
12. तस्मिन् सति इदमस्तीति कार्यकारणताऽपि या।
साऽप्यपेक्षाविहीनानां जडानां नोपपद्यते॥
13. योगिनामपि मृद्बीजे विनैवेच्छावशेन तत्।
घटादि जायते तत्तत् स्थिर-स्वार्थ-क्रियाकरम्॥ I.P. II. 4-10
14. निरुपादानसम्भारमभिन्तानेव तन्यते।
जगच्चित्रं नमस्तस्मै कलानाथाय शूलिने॥
Abhinava attributes this to Vasugupta but is untraced in latter's works.
15. एष प्रमाता मायान्ध: संसारी कर्मबन्धन:।
विद्याभिज्ञापितैश्वर्यश्चिद्घनो मुक्त उच्यने॥ I.P. III. 2
16. मेयं साधारणं मुक्त: स्वात्माभेदेन मन्यते।
महेश्वरो यथा बद्ध: पुनरत्यन्तभेदवत्॥ I.P. IV. 1-13
17. तैस्तैरप्युपयाचितैरुपनतस्तन्व्या:
स्थितोऽप्यन्तिके।
कान्तो लोकसमान एवमपरिज्ञातो न रंतुं यथा।
लोकस्यैष तथानवेक्षितगुण: स्वात्मापि विश्वेश्वरो
नैवालं निजवैभवाय तदियं तत्प्रत्यभिज्ञोदिता॥ I.P. IV. 1-17

---

*Reading in the original text is कायाश्रिता.

Epilogue

1. शक्ति-संकोचादयस्तु यद्यपि प्रत्यभिज्ञायां न प्रतिपादिताः, तथापि आम्नायिकत्वादस्माभिः प्रदर्श्यन्ते। —क्षेम on PH. Sūtra 18
2. अत एव ये सदा एतत् (पञ्चविधकृत्यं) परिशीलयन्ति, ते स्वरूप-विकल्पमयं विश्वं जानाना जीवन्मुक्ता इति आम्नाताः। —प्रह. सू· 50 Com.
3. प्रकाशैकघनः परो (=शिवः)यःस एवाहं, स चाहमेव, न तु अन्यःकश्चित् अत्तो विकल्प-सृष्टिरपि मम स्वातन्त्र्यलक्षणः विभवः- इत्येवं विमर्शे दृढीभूते सत्यपरिक्षीणविकल्पोऽपि जीवन्नेव मुक्तः। —अभिनव on IP. IV. 1-12
4. चिदानन्दभूतः शिवोऽहं शिवोऽहम्।

Glossary of Sanskrit Terms

A

A	symbol of Śiva.
Ābhāsana	Appearance; (Esoteric meaning) Sṛṣṭi – creation.
Adhaḥ-kuṇḍalinī	The field of *Kuṇḍalinī* from *Laṁbikā* to one-three-fourth of her coils in the *Mūlādhāra Cakra.*
Adho-vaktra	*Meḍhra Kanda* situated at the root of the rectum.
Ādi-koṭi	The starting point of breath; *hṛt*; the length of a breath is measured from that point in the heart.
Ahaṁbhāva—Ahantā	I-consciousness; 'I-ness'.
Akhyāti	Ignorance.
Akula	Śiva.
Alaṁ-grāsa	Bringing experienced object to the sameness with the conscience of the Self (see the note concerned).
Amāyīya	Beyond the scope of Māyā e.g. *Amāyīya śabda* – A word the meaning of which does not depend on convention. The word and the designated object are identical.
Anacka (an-ac-ka)	(i) Uttering the consonant without a vowel, (ii) esoteric meaning: concentrating on any *mantra* back to the source of its utterance.
Anāhata	Inner spiritual sound.
Ānanda	Bliss.
Anāśrita Śiva	The state of Śiva in which the universe is negated to him.
Āṇava mala	*Mala* pertaining to *aṇu.* Innate ignorance of the Jīvātman. Primary limiting condition which reduces the universal consciousness

	of the soul and brings a sense of imperfection in him.
Anta koṭi	The last edge of exhaled breath at a distance of twelve *aṅgulas.* Simply called *Dvādaśa.*
Antarmukhībhāva	Introversion of consciousness.
Aṇu	The limited empirical individual.
Anuttara	The Highest: From whom there is none higher.
Apāna	The vital breath that goes down to the *anus.*
Apavarga	Mokṣa, liberation from *Saṁsāra.*
Artha	Aim, end; object.
Āśyānatā	Shrunken stage, solidification.
Ātma-viśrānti	Resting on the self.

B

Bahir-mukhatā	extroversion of consciousness.
Baindavīkalā	Will-power (kalā) pertaining to *Bindu* (to knower). The freedom of Parama Śiva whereby the knower always remains the knower.
Bala	Power, *Cid-bala* – power of true self or universal consciousness.
Bandha	(1) bondage; (2) a certain yogic pose of the body.
Bhairava	Parama Śiva, the Highest Reality – this acronym consists of *bha - bharaṇa* - maintenance of the world; *ra - ravaṇa* – the destruction or withdrawal of the world; *va - vamana* – projection or creation of the world.
Bhairavī mudrā	a posture in which the gaze is turned outward without winking of the eyes while attention is turned inward.
Bhāva	an object; existence both internal and external.
Bhoga	experience; enjoyment.
Bhrū-madhya	the centre between two eyebrows.
Bhūcarī	sub-species of Vāmeśvarī; it is concerned with *bhāvas* or existent objects; bhū – existence; Existent objects are the sphere of *bhūcarī.*
Bhūmikā	role, the part to be played.
Bhuvana	plane of existence, world.

Bodha	enlightenment.
Bījāvasthāpana	setting the seed; (esoterically) concealment of the true nature.
Bindu	a metaphysical point, *ghanībhūta śakti* – the compact mass of Śakti gathered into an undifferentiated point ready for creation. (1) *paraḥ pramātā* – the highest self of consciousness. The *anusvāra* – symbolized as a dot (.) to express the indivisibility of Śiva despite creation or manifestation of the universe.
Brahma-nāḍī	Suṣumṇā Nāḍī.
Brahmarandhra	the *Sahasrāra Cakra.* (1) cerebral aperture through which the soul of a Yogī passes to merge into Brahman.
Buddhi	Intelligence, Super-personal mind.

C

Caitanya	Absolute consciousness characterised by *Svātantrya,* Jñāna and Kriyā.
Cakra	centre of Prāṇic energy. There are six *Cakras* in the body.
Camatkāra	(1) bliss of pure I-consciousness. (2) delight of artistic expression.
Carama kalā	Śāntātīta kalā.
Cetana	self; parama Śiva.
Cetya	knowable, object of consciousness.
Cheda	cessation of breath by sounding *anacka* sounds.
Cidānanda	(*lit*) consciousness and bliss; the nature of the ultimate Reality.
Cit	foundational consciousness; the Absolute unchanging principle of all changes.
Citi	the power of the Absolute, the author of the world process.
Citi-cakra	*Saṁvit-cakra.*
Citta	Individual mind.

D

Darśana	A system of philosophy.
Dārḍhya	firmness of mind or concentration.

Deśa	space, region.
Dhyāna	meditation.
Dik-carī	sub-species of *Vāmeśvarī*, connected with outer senses (outer senses are concerned with space or *dik*).
Dvādaśānta	distance of 12 *aṅgulas* (fingers) from the tip of the nose in outer space; exhalation is supposed to reach this distance.

G

Gocarī	sub-species of *Vāmeśvarī*, connected with *antaḥkaraṇa* (inward sense, mind); *Go*=sense.
Grāhaka	knower, subject.
Grāhya	known, object.

H

Ha	symbol of Śakti.
Haṭha pāka	persistent process of assimilating experience to the consciousness of the Experient.
Haṁsa	the *prāṇa-apāna* breath.
Hetu	cause.
Hetumat	effect.
Hṛdaya	heart, a mystic centre (in the region of the heart), central consciousness (in Yoga).

I

Icchā	Will, the Śakti of Sadāśiva.
Idantā	'This-ness', This-consciousness, objectivity.
Indriya	a sense-organ.
Īsvara Tattva	the fourth state down from Śiva, the consciousness: 'This am I'.

J

Jagadānanda	(i) The bliss of the self or Divine appearing as universe (ii) the bliss of Divine made visible.
Jagat	the world process.
Jāgrat	the waking condition.
Jīvan-mukti	liberation while one is alive.

Jñāna	knowledge, spiritual realization, the Śakti of Śiva.

K

Kalā	limited agency, creativity, part of a letter or word as in *ha-kalā paryantam.*
Kāla	time; Śakti or power determining succession.
Kālāgni	the lowest *bhuvana* or plane of existence in Nivṛtti Kalā.
Kālāgni-Rudra	universal destructive fire.
Kañcuka	covering of Māyā. They are five in number.
Karaṇeśvaryaḥ	Khecarī, Gocarī, Dikcarī and Bhūcarī *cakras* (groups of these Śaktis).
Kārma mala	Mala due to Karmas.
Kārya	effect.
Khecarī	a sub-species of *Vāmeśvari śakti* connected with Pramātā (*Lit.* one who moves in *Kha* i.e *ākāśa,* a symbol of consciousness).
Khecarī Mudrā	in this *mudrā,* eyes are wide open, gaze outside with no winking of eyes, but the concentration is inward.
Khyāti	Jñāna, knowledge.
Kriyā	action, the Śakti of Śuddha Vidyā.
Kṣobha	agitation.
Kula	Śakti.
Kulāmnāya	the Śākta system or doctrine.

L

Laya and *nilaya*	absorption.

M

Madhya	the central consciousness, *Saṁvit,* Suṣumṇā nāḍī.
Madhya dhāma	susumṇā nāḍī, Brahma – nāḍī.
Madhyamā	*śabda* in a subtle form (existing in the mind prior to its gross manifestation).
Madhya śakti	*Saṁvit śakti.*
Māheśvarya	the power of Maheśvara.
Mala	dross, ignorance, *Pāśa.*

Mantra	(i) the experient who has realized the *Śuddha Vidyā*. (ii) sacred words for chanting and meditation.
Mantra–Maheśvara	experient who has realized Sadāśiva Tattva
Māyā	(i) limiting principle of the Divine. (ii) source of five Kañcukas.
Māyā-pramātā	the empirical self, governed by Māyā.
Māyīya Mala	Mala pertaining to Māyā.
Meya (Prameya)	object.
Mudrā	(i) that which gives the bliss of spiritual consciousness (ii) Yogic control of certain organs as a help in concentration.
Mudrā Krama or *Krama Mudrā*	the condition of mind in which by the force of *samāveśa,* the mind swings alternatively between the internal (self or Śiva) and the external (the world) which now appears as Śiva.

N

Nāda	internal spontaneous sound.
Nāda-bindu	the first creative pulsation and its compact mass: Śakti and Śiva.
Nādānta	subtle energy of Prāṇana.
Nibhālana	perception.
Nimeṣa	closing of eyelids; dissolution of the world.
Nimīlana samādhi	the meditative condition in which the individual consciousness gets absorbed into the Universal Consciousness.
Nirāśraya	without any support.
Nirvikalpa	higher consciousness free from thought-constructs.
Niṣkala	partless Śiva above manifestation or creation.
Nityatva	eternity.
Niyati	limitation by cause-effect relation, spatial limitation.

P

Pañcarātra	the philosophy of Vaiṣṇavism.
Para	highest.

Para-pramātā	the highest experient; parama Śiva.
Parāmarśa	(i) Comprehension (ii) seizing mentally (iii) experience.
Parāpara	both identical and different, unity in diversity, intermediate stage.
Parā-śakti	the divine Śakti, *Citi*.
Parā vāk	Vibrating movement of the Divine, the unmanifest Śakti.
Pari-cchinna	eliminated.
Pariṇāma	transformation.
Paramārtha	the highest reality; the highest goal.
Pāśa	bondage.
Paśu	one who is bound, individual soul.
Paśyantī	the divine view of the universe in undifferentiated form; *Vāk śakti* – going forth as 'seeing' – ready to create words in which there is no difference between *Vācya* and *Vācaka*.
Pati	Lord Śiva.
Pati-deśa	Śivahood, the state of liberation.
Prakāśa	light, principle of self-revelation; principle by which everything is known.
Prakṛti	source of objectivity (from *Buddhi* down to the earth).
Pralayākala or *Pralayakevalin*	resting in the Māyā-tattva, not cognisant of anything.
Pramāṇa	means of knowing, proof.
Pramātā	the knower, the experient, the subject.
Prameya	object of knowledge, known object.
Prāṇa	vital air, vital energy, the vital Vāyu while expiration.
Prasara	(*Lit.* expansion) – manifestation of Śiva in the form of the universe through his Śakti.
Prathā	the mode of appearance, the way.
Pratyabhijñā	recognition.
Pratyāhāra	(In Yoga) withdrawal of the senses from their objects.
Pūrṇāhantā	the perfect I-consciousness, non-relational I-consciousness.

Puryaṣṭaka	(i) city of eight (viz five *tanmāttras,* buddhi, ahaṁkāra and manas) (ii) *liṅga* Śarīra.

R

Rāga	(i) passion (ii) a kañcuka of Māyā which creates desire.
Rajas	(i) the principle of motion, activity and disharmony (ii) a *guṇa,* constituent of Prakṛti.
Rakti	relish, enjoyment (esoteric meaning - '*sthiti*' – maintenance).

S

Śabda-brahman	ultimate reality in the form of vibration of which human word is a gross representation. In this state, thought and word are identical.
Śabda-rāśi	totality of words.
Sadāśiva or *Sādākhya*	the third tattva below Śiva. Icchā or Will is predominant in this Tattva.
Sahaja	natural (from the point of view of the Universal Consciousness).
Sakala	all the jivas involved in Māyā. They have no knowledge of their Śivahood.
Śakti-pāta	Descent of the divine Śakti; grace.
Śakti-prasara or *śakti-vikāsa*	retention of the experience of the *samādhi* after emergence to normalcy.
Śakti-saṅkoca	withdrawal of attention from sense-activity and turning it towards the inner reality.
Śakti-vikāsa	concentration of attention on the inner consciousness even when the senses are open to their respective objects.
Śakti-viśrānti	merging back into *samādhi* and resting in that condition.
Samādhi	collectedness of mind; mental absorption.
Samāna	the vital Vāyu helpful in assimilation of food etc; brings about equilibrium between Prāṇa and Apāna.
Samāpatti	*samādhi,* attainment of psychic at-one-ment, consummation.
Samarasa	having the same feeling or consciousness.

Sāmarasya	identity of consciousness, union of Śiva and Śakti.
Saṁkalpa	resolve.
Samāveśa	(i) being possessed of the divine. (ii) absorption of the individual consciousness into the divine.
Saṁhāra	reabsorption, withdrawal.
Saṁsāra or *saṁsṛṣṭi*	transmigratory existence, world process.
Saṁskāra	residual traces of the mind in the subconsciousness.
Saṁvit	Consciousness, supreme consciousness.
Saṁvit-devatā	(i) from macrocosmic point of view : *Devatās* viz. *Khecarī, gocarī, dikcarī* and *bhūcarī*. (ii) from microcosmic point of view : internal and external senses.
Sarva-kartṛtva	omnipotence.
Ṣaṣṭha-vaktra	(*Lit.* the sixth organ) *Meḍhra kanda* near the root of the rectum.
Sattva	(i) the principle of being, light and harmony (ii) a constituent of Prakṛti.
Śiva-tattva	the first tattva whose main characteristic is *Cit.*
Śuddha Vidyā or *Vidyā*	the 5th tattva Śiva. In this stage, 'I' and 'This' are equally prominent. *Kriyā* is prominent. The consciousness at this stage is "I am I and also This".
Śuddhādhvan	the pure path; extra-mundane existence; manifestation of the first five tattvas viz. Śiva, Śakti, Sadāśiva, Īśvara, Śuddha vidyā.
Śūnya	void; the state in which no object is experienced.
Śūnya-pramātā-pralayākala	having the experience of the void.
Svarūpāpatti	attainment of one's own real nature or True Self.
Svatantra	of absolute or unimpaired will.
Svātantrya – or *Svecchā*	the Absolute Will of the Supreme.
Svātmasāt-kṛ	to assimilate to oneself; to integrate to oneself.

T

Tamas	principle of inertia and delusion–a constituent of Prakṛti.

Tanutā reduction; becoming less gradually; subtleness.

Tattva that-ness, the very being of a thing; principle.

Tantra science of cosmic principle, a revealed work.

Trika the system of philosophy of the triad – (i) Śiva, Sakti, Nara (the bound soul). (ii) Para (the highest), having to do with identity, *Parāpara* (identity in difference) and *apara* (difference and the sense of difference).

Turīya or *Tūryā* The fourth state of consciousness beyond the state of waking, dreaming and deep sleep and stringing together all these states; the metaphysical self, distinct from empirical self; the *sākṣī* or witnessing consciousness.

Turyātita the state of consciousness transcending the Turīya state, the state annulling the distinction between waking, dreaming and deep sleep.

U

Udāna the vital Vāyu, the *śakti* that moves up in suṣumṇā at spiritual awakening

Unmeṣa (i) (*Lit.* opening of the eyes) the start of the world process. (ii) In Śaiva Yoga – unfolding of the spiritual consciousness by concentrating in the inner consciousness.

Unmīlana unfolding; manifestation.

Unmīlana samādhi the state of mind in which even with open eyes the world appears to be Śiva.

Upādāna material cause.

Upādhi limiting adjunct.

Ūrdhva–Kuṇḍalinī the risen up *kuṇḍalinī* when Prāṇa and Apāna enter Suṣumṇā.

V

Vācaka word, the indicator.

Vācya object, the indicated referent.

Vāha the Prāṇa flowing in Iḍā and Piṅgalā Nāḍīs.

Vahni (Śaiva Yoga) entering completely into the root and half of the middle of *adhaḥ kuṇḍalinī*.

Vaikharī — Śakti as gross physical word.

Vāmeśvarī — the divine Śakti that 'vomits' or sends forth the universe out of the Absolute. It produces the reverse (*Vāma*) consciousness of difference (the Absolute is differenceless).

Vibhūti — power, splendour.

Vidyā — limited knowledge.

Vigraha — individual form or shape, body.

Vijñāna kala — the experient below Śuddha Vidyā but above Māyā. He is free from Kārma and Māyā *malas*.

Vikalpa — difference of perception, diversity ideation, imagination.

Vikalpa-kṣaya — the dissolution of *vikalpas*.

Vikalpana — the differention-making activity of the mind.

Vilāpana — dissolution (esoterically – *anugraha* – grace).

Vilaya — concealment.

Vimarśa — *Lit.* experience. Technically – the self-consciousness of the Supreme, full of Jñāna and Kriyā bringing about the world process.

Vimarśana — intuitive awareness; technically—*saṁhāra,* absorption.

Viṣa — from √viṣ—to pervade; (technical in Śaiva Yoga)—entering into the remaining half and wholly into the top of *adhaḥ kuṇḍalinī* right upto the position where *Ūrdhva-kuṇḍalinī* ends.

Viśvamaya or *Viśvātmaka* — immanent.

Viśvottirṇa — transcendent.

Vyāmohitatā — delusion.

Vyāna — the vital Vāyu that is everywhere; pervasive prāṇa.

Vyāpakatva — all-pervasiveness.

Vyutthāna — *Lit.* 'rising', coming to normal consciousness after contemplation or *samādhi.*

Bibliography

Abhinavagupta : *Tantra-sāra,* Kashmir Sanskrit Series (KSS), Srinagar, 1918.

———, *Tantrāloka* (with Jayaratha's commentary (KSS).

———, *Paramārtha-sāra* (Comm. by Yogarāja): KSS 7, 1916.

Ādyanātha: *Anuttara-pañcāśikā*: KSS 14, 1918.

Bhagavadgītā, (with 11 Comm.) Gujarati Printing Press, 1935.

Bhandarkar, R. G.: *Vaiṣṇavism and Saivism* (A Symposium), Bhandarkar O. R. Institute, Pune, 1976.

Bharatiya Vidya Bhavan: *Vedic Age* (History and Culture of Indian People), Bombay, 1965.

Chatterji, J.C. – *Kashmir Śaivism,* Kashmir Grantha Mala, Śrinagar 1914.

Dasgupta, S.N.: *History of Indian Philosophy,* Vol. V, Motilal Banarsidass, Delhi, 1975.

Hastings: *Encyclopaedia of Religion and Ethics.*

Jash, Prabanananda: *History of Śaivism,* Roy and Choudhuri, Calcutta, 1974.

Kṣemaraja: *Parā-prāveśikā,* KSS, 1918.

———, *Pratyabhijñā-hṛdaya,* Jayadev Singh(ed.), Motilal Banarsidass, Delhi, 1980.

Mādhavācārya – *Śāṅkara-digvijaya* (with Comm. *Ḍiṇḍima*), Sarva-darśana-saṅgraha. Anandashrama, Pune, 1964.

Mahābhārata – Gītā Press, Gorakhpur.

Mahā-Śiva Purāṇa – Pandit Pustakalaya, Varanasi, Samvat 2020.

Mahesvarānanda: *Mahārtha-Mañjarī,* Yoga Tantra Granthmala, Varanasi, 1972.

Pandey, K.C.: *Abhinavagupta: An Historical and Philosophical Study,* Chowkhamba Sanskrit Series, Banaras, 1935.

———, *Bhāskarī,* Vol. I, III, Lucknow University.

Pandit, B.N.: *Aspects of Kashmir Śaivism,* Utpala Pub., Srinagar, 1977.

Patañjali: *Vyākaraṇa-mahā-bhāṣya,* ed. by Keilhorn.

Purāṇas: Guru Mandal edition, Calcutta.

Radhakrishnan, S. (ed.): *History of Philosophy – Eastern and Western*, Vol. I, George Allen & Unwin, London, 1967.
Ramakrishna Mission: *Cultural Heritage of India*, Vol. IV, Calcutta, 1956.
Śaṅkara: *Sārīraka Bhāṣya* (on Brahma Sūtra), Nirnaya Sagara, Bombay, 1904.
Ṣaṭ-triṁśat-sandoha (Comm. Rājānakānanda) KSS 13, Srinagar, 1916.
Sinha,–*Schools of Śaivism*, Sinha Publishing House, Calcutta, 1970.
Smṛtis: Guru Mandal edition, Calcutta.
Somānanda – *Śivadṛṣṭi*, KSS 54, 1934.
Tagare, G.V.: Śaivadarśana (Marathi), Continental, Pune, 1987.
Upaniṣat-Saṅgraha: J.L. Shastri(ed.), Motilal Banarsidass, Delhi, 1970.
Utpaladeva : *Īśvara-pratyabhijñā* (Comm. by Abhinavagupta), Vol. I, KSS 22, 1918; Vol. II, KSS 33, 1921.
Vasugupta : *Śivasūtra*, G.V. Tagare [ed. and tr. (Marathi)], Impressions, Belgaum, 1996.
———, *Spanda Kārikā*, G.V. Tagare [ed. and tr. (Marathi)], Satara, 1984
Vedas : Svādhyāya Maṇḍala, Aundh.

Index